$5⁰⁰±

#10

THIS WAY, MISS

George Jessel

THIS WAY,
MISS

With a foreword by WILLIAM SAROYAN

Illustrated with photographs

HENRY HOLT AND COMPANY, NEW YORK

For Jerilynn—

I shall watch over thee well, so that no cruel winter frost nor torrid desert winds halt thy springtime bloom. . . .

Foreword

THE MASTER OF WIT is not to be taken lightly. He is apt to be a provoker of laughter among crowds altogether from having known the profoundest brooding and even despair of the solitary soul. Somewhere in this rather wonderful and always-challenging book, George Jessel, wearing cap and bells of the clown and boots and belt of an ancient clergy, remarks, "Men find that as they make ready to play the last act in their span of life, they're inclined to find their eyes well up with tears at the least provocation. I remember the late Sam Bernard would cry like a child if you shuffled a pack of cards. The ace of spades reminded him of his father and the queen of hearts brought to mind a girl who was drowned." Tears, tears, mysterious and tender and angry tears, even while the living voice is decorated with all of the varied ornaments of raffish laughter—and a whole room at the Waldorf-Astoria responds as shade to sun, for that man is up there again, speaking with his own peculiar inflection and rhythm, as if he were still singing a magnificent and mournful dirge in a child's synagogue of long-ago New York, or a ballad of heartbreak and love about a mother's eyes on the stage of a theater five miles and ten years from the synagogue—for Jessel's speech, as nasal as it may be, as the admirers and imitators and parodists have permitted us to know, is a form of song, of chant, a mingling of that affectionate sorrow and jaunty laughter which is the proud cloak of the children of Israel.

So far I have never been at a dinner at which, at the almost inevitable and predictable moment, George Jessel has been called upon to say a few words for the living or for the dead, but neither has the reader, most likely; and yet in reading the words in this book, many of which he has spoken at such events, I have been able to hear him quite clearly, as I am sure the reader will be able to hear him.

As far as I know, there has never before been a book like this book, perhaps for the simple reason that there has never before been a man like George Jessel. The book contains many of his talks at all kinds of affairs, on all kinds of occasions. In addition to these talks the book contains a father's report to a daughter—about the world, about the quarrels among men, about the father himself—who he is, how he has lived, and why he is who he is and has lived as he has lived. The father's purpose is to indicate a way for the daughter— a way of life, a way of faith, a way of intelligence, humor, grace, earnestness, and love.

But if I have never been at a Jessel dinner, I have met him from time to time for a moment over the past ten or fifteen years, and I remember him and the quality which distinguishes him. Jessel is the man whose nature is too swift and gallant for anything other than amused but profound courtesy, not to others alone but to life itself. The quality that distinguishes him is speed and aptness, to the end that righteousness shall not be dull, virtue tiresome, faith uncharitable, or life itself weary. Even so, now and then, even Jessel falters for a moment, and there is a flash of regrettable hatred and temporary forfeiture of intelligence and grace—which I shall not permit myself to point out specifically, leaving the matter entirely to Jessel himself and to the reader. As far as I am concerned, such flaws enhance the man's achievement, which is profoundly personal and yet essentially public.

Who is Jessel? What is his achievement? In a brief foreword it is not for me to seek to answer such complex questions. They are asked, rather, to impel the biographer into action, for I am sure an account of George Jessel must come to pass and take its place among the accounts of all distinguished Americans.

This book constitutes volume two of his own account of George Jessel. I consider it an ever richer account than volume one, entitled *So Help Me*. Volume three should be along in due time.

In the meantime, here he is—Mr. George Jessel himself.

WILLIAM SAROYAN

Contents

THIS WAY, MISS

1. Overture

So that there may be no confusion as to the significance of the title of this book, *This Way, Miss* is a series of essays intended for my daughter Jerilynn, giving her the opinions which I have formed about life in general, and particularly the events in my own since she was born—the people I have met, the places I've been—from Roosevelt to Rubirosa, from Liverpool to Liberace. I have mingled with presidents, senators, governors, majors, actors, authors, composers, crooners, gangsters, glamour girls, geniuses, and mixed-up people.

When my child was a year old, I finished a book called *So Help Me*. It was published by my dear friend Bennett Cerf, famous as a guesser on the television program *What's My Line,* and as a collector of other people's jokes. My book enjoyed many printings. It was the story of my life from the beginning to the age of forty-two. It was very frankly written, with no holds barred, nor curtains drawn. This tome was born at a time when I was breathing happily again after having had some six years' violent depression, such as being in jail for shooting a man, having failure after failure in almost all facets of the amusement business, and then, in a moment of amorous abandon, walking through the arches of connubial felicity with a young lady just sweet sixteen. She very wisely gave me back to the theater, from which I have never been divorced, and graced my life by giving me a baby girl,

Jerilynn who, as I write this, is nearing thirteen and shows every promise of being a great comfort to me in the twilight years.

So, I am hoping that this book will serve as an emotional map for her to study, and that she will be able to benefit by my observations, or at least be amused.

2. A Few Words in the Wings

I THINK OF YOU, Jeri, when you were not quite two, and we were just getting acquainted.

I did not know much about getting along with such a little person. I had only known one, my brother Edward Aaron Jessel.

So before we go on, let me go back and tell you about him—and just a little of my childhood which was over at nine and a half when I went away from home to go on the stage.

I have never known a smarter and more sensitive child than Edward, my brother. He was aged a year and eleven months when he passed away. Of all the most advanced children of today who know all the TV commercials by heart, none that I have ever seen or heard compares to Edward. He was but a year and ten months old when I was taken ill with scarlet fever, and that particular illness wasn't quite as easy to cure in 1907 as it is now. I was very sick, and little Edward would crawl toward the door of my room, and I could hear him whisper, "Poor Albie. I'm so sorry you're sick, but you'll be better soon." He called me Albie, which was an abbreviation for my middle name, Albert, which my grandmother stuck in; and she and all of my mother's family called me Albie, because Grandma thought George was much too stylish and she could find no Hebrew equivalent for it.

When Edward was eighteen months old, he knew that Grandma was blind, and when he heard her come through the railroad flat we lived in, and he was playing on the floor, he would say, "Grandma, please don't step on me. I know you can't see." And while I was convalescing from the fever, they fed me ice cream, and I evidently wasn't quite as clear of the germs as the doctors thought, for little Edward licked off brother Albie's plate, and within a few days he was gone.

Albie's a kind of an odd name, a much warmer-sounding name than Georgie, I think; and I wonder what Grandma would have thought if she had lived long enough to see the mass move of the people from the east side to Washington Heights where the newly born were soon to be named Montmorency Cohen, De Witt Clinton Fink, T. Hemisphere Rabinowitz; and one baby boy was even christened St. Albans Court Levine, having been born on the first floor of the apartment house, St. Alban's Court, on 123rd Street.

As I am writing this, Jeri, you are nearby, reading *Gone with the Wind*. And you are not listening when I speak to you. But did I ever tell you that I actually saw Theodore Roosevelt in person? And even though in my earlier days I saw pictures of Admiral Dewey, the hero of Manila, in almost everybody's house, I have never seen a man walk with such pride and such authority as my Grandpa did when he led the May Party my mother gave me when I was eight. We marched. From 116th to Fifth Avenue to 120th into Mount Morris Park. But despite the fun of the May Party, it had a note of sadness because a few days before, I had buried our canary in a candy box on a little hill right near where the Maypole stood. So that's why I know exactly how you felt, at six, when they told you your little duck had gone to sleep and would never wake up again.

Maybe it is best that you do not hear what I am thinking. You're a pretty hep kid, and as you often tell me, "Daddy, that is awfully corny!" Well, maybe so, but we are an awfully long way from home. We are up in an airplane flying from Jerusalem to Rome, and your father is at that stage of the game when men feel closer to the past, and their minds become like museums of memories and all sorts of little thoughts turn up.

I am thinking of when I was a kid in Harlem, where people didn't have dogs or cats as pets. If there was enough food for a dog, it was given to a relative who had newly arrived, and I feel certain that everybody from 110th Street to 120th was afraid of a dog, with the exception of Schultz, our janitor, who feared only his wife and the Kaiser.

A few months after the May Party, my mother, Charlotte, was completely without funds. My illness and then little Eddie's had cleaned out the money my father had left, and Mother went to work as a cashier, or ticket seller, in the Imperial Theater on 116th Street, owned by a man called Clarence McKibbon. It was because of her working at the nickelodeon, as it was called, that my schoolmates Walter Winchell and Jack Wiener and I were able to get in free. And she arranged that we sing for McKibbon, and we became the Imperial Trio. I've told you about how we all went with the Gus Edwards Troupe, and the heartbreaking trials and tribulations with the Gerry Society, which refused to let me work in most of the big cities on account of my age. And in *So Help Me*, I wrote about getting a phony birth certificate with the name "Imroe Carsany" which I used when I was ten, and the birth certificate made me twenty-three. However, the long pants, the almost basso-profundo voice, and the unlit cigar fooled everybody and the midget was okay to go on.

Yes, I was twelve years old, and I don't think anything can tell you better how the times have changed than the fact that at that age I appeared in fourteen performances a week in the vaudeville act, "Gus Edwards' Song Revue"; played many parts throughout; sold music during the intermission; and with Lou Silvers at the piano, who was Gus' musical director, would visit small cafés at night and plug Gus Edwards' songs: "Look Out for Jimmy Valentine," "If I Was a Millionaire," "Lucy Anna Lou," and others. Sometimes this would go on until two or three o'clock in the morning. For all this I got fifteen dollars a week—eleven for my acting, a dollar for selling the music, and three dollars for the midnight plugs. And you, Jeri, in your twelfth year, have appeared several times on television and for two and a half minutes' work you received five hundred dollars. The only thing that makes us alike is that I didn't have anything left out of the fifteen dollars I got, and you don't have anything left out of the five hundred.

As I look at you across the aisle with your seat belt strapped tight around you and your head deep in your book, I can't help thinking of my brother Edward again—for you remember, I showed you that one little picture I have, and you look so much like him. So I guess that it is him I am lonesome for, right this minute. It is a shame he could not have stayed on longer. I think I had better start reading some more books on faith. I don't want ever for you and me to believe that my brother is completely lost. No, by God, I refuse to believe that anything is lost. There must be a reason for everything, and it must be that everything that is alive lives, and lives, and relives. A breathing barnacle might have become Moses, a long-since-departed eagle might have become Einstein, and a starling frozen to a telegraph wire might have become Judy Garland . . . Eternal law, eternal life!

3. Curtain Going Up

I AM NOT QUITE SURE, my child, that I believe in heredity, or that the sins or virtues of the father are visited upon the children. Many great ball players have had kids who could not learn, or had no desire to put on a baseball glove. My aunt Debbie was the most wonderful cook, and her daughter had a tough time preparing corn flakes and cream.

But as far as you are concerned, I believe you are destined to be in the theatrical profession, for if ever a kid had more of a show-business conception than you, I'd like to hear about it.

Now, despite the fact that your mother and I are the best of friends—even better than that, for I love her as I would my closest of kin—when we were married we did not get along any too well. I was not too successful, and was irritable and hard to get along with. And your mother and I were going to split up. We were in Florida together and had decided to go our separate ways one particular night. Then I picked up a paper and read that Walter Winchell had said that we were getting along well, and ham that I was, I called your mother up and said, "Lois, we can't split up now with what Winchell said."

We went back together that night, and a few weeks later we found out that Lois was going to have a baby. I was playing personal appearances throughout the country in what was left of vaudeville houses, and your mother played with me. The billing was: "IN PERSON, GEORGE JESSEL—with Lois Andrews (Mrs. George Jessel)."

In March, 1941, when your mother had been carrying you for more than two months, we were booked to play the State Lake Theatre in Chicago, which was a motion picture and vaudeville house. We gave four or five performances a day, the first show starting around ten o'clock in the morning. Around eleven o'clock I went on stage. The audience was not very appreciative in the early morning. It was made up of some kids who were playing hooky from school, women waiting for some particular shop to open or having a date later somewhere in the Loop, a lot of roustabouts who had nothing else to do or were waiting for the poolrooms to open, and also a bunch of city salesmen who had been out on the town for an hour or two, couldn't make any sales and were coming into the theater disgruntled, putting their sample cases under the seats, and getting mad at the actors on the stage, because they were earning a living.

Anyway, I came on, told a few gags, and introduced your mother. She entered and there was always a "ooh-ooh-ooh" and a wolf whistle or two when she came on. She was only seventeen, and as pretty a girl as there has ever been. She got as far as the chorus of her first song and then collapsed on the stage. I ran out, accompanied by one of the stage-hands. She was carried to her dressing room. I ran back on stage and asked if there was a doctor in the house.

By the time I ran back to the dressing room, there was a doctor there. As good fortune would have it, my best pal in Chicago, Paul Montague, had gone to his doctor that morning and had taken the doctor to see my first show. Dr. Wolfson, it was. Your mother had had a hemorrhage.

Within ten minutes we had her back in the hotel, and the doctor prescribed complete rest. Your mother had to lie in bed with her feet held high by an apparatus that was attached to the ceiling. For ten days she lay there, rehearsing songs, planning costumes, reading theatrical magazines, and some months later, you were born, in Los Angeles, California.

I was playing in Philadelphia at the time, and the news of your arrival was brought to me while I was on the stage playing a scene. One of the men of my company, Selden Bennett, whispered in my ear while the audience was laughing at a gag. He said, "Work fast, you have just had a little girl, and you ought to get your Mrs. on the phone."

When I came off the stage, I ran to the hotel in my make-up and called your grandmother. At the end of the week in Philadelphia I took a midnight plane to fly out to see you.

Six weeks later your mother flew to New York and brought you right out on the stage while I was singing a song.

So, baby, you may not turn out to be a Barrymore, a Hayes, a Cornell, or a Hepburn (Audrey or Katharine, I am not particular), but you were certainly to the theater born, no matter what you choose to be.

4. End of an Act

ABOUT A YEAR LATER, Jeri darling, your mother and I agreed to be divorced. She had taken you back to California some months before, and no two people can have a happy married life with a difference of twenty-five hundred miles between them, and also a difference of twenty-five years.

I came out to California to see you, and one morning read a newspaper headline that everything was over between your mom and me, and although I had been sure that I wouldn't be hurt, I was.

It took me quite some time to get over it. I then opened in a little revue in Los Angeles, and then later in New York in *Showtime,* and, for a change, made a big hit.

One morning Arthur Freed, MGM's great musical producer, sent for me with the idea to bring me out to Hollywood as an actor and a writer. This was very attractive to me, because I wanted to see you so badly, but I told Arthur that at the moment I would rather stay on Broadway, as I had not fared too well in Hollywood before. I think this is rather an understatement—I had been fired by nearly every one of the studios on one or more occasion. Anyway I said I would think it over. Coming down in the hotel elevator, I bumped into Joseph M. Schenck who, with Darryl Zanuck, headed Twentieth Century-Fox Studios. Joe and I had always been good friends, had always had a great deal in common—including the same ex-wife, Norma Talmadge, to whom we are still devoted. He also wanted me to come to Hollywood to write and appear in a motion picture about vaudeville, but he said, "I am leaving for the Coast tonight, and Darryl Zanuck will talk to you. He is coming out of the Army—he will be in New York for a few days and see your show."

A short time later Colonel Zanuck (he was still in uniform) came in to see my show, and we had supper together. Strangely, and to my good fortune, he had read my book *So Help Me* coming up on the train and had enjoyed it. We met again the next night, and he again came to the theater. While our conversations had not included just when I was to go to Hollywood and what I was to do, I felt sure that there was a deal in the making for me to act in motion pictures at Twentieth Century-Fox. For I had watched Zanuck in the audience while I was playing, and saw him laugh heartily at my character, "Professor Larbermacher." I made notes to be sure and bring all my material and costumes out of the storehouse so that I would be ready for any acting emergency.

That night we had supper again, and before I got a chance to talk about all kinds of parts I wanted to play, Darryl said to me, "Georgie, I enjoyed you very much tonight. You're awfully funny. Now how would you like to get rid of all those funny clothes and wigs, and sit behind a desk and try to produce motion pictures? I'll give you a good chance. I'll give you a two-year contract. You will work very close to me and I think you will be good at it. See Joe Moscowitz in our New York office—I am sure we will make a deal."

I was as completely surprised as if someone had said to me, "I love the way you sing 'My Mother's Eyes'—you should be president of a bank." I called all of my cronies—and you must know that all personalities in show business have a set of cronies. The insensitive call these fellow "stooges," but it's never been so in my case. The half-dozen close comrades I have around me were around with me since I was sixteen years of age. Or better still, I was around with them when I was sixteen. In order of their seniority, these are as follows:

"Doc"—we met when we were both nine. He was a Cockney kid from the East End of London. He came to sit beside me during the few months I was at school. Because of his strange accent, all the tough kids around wanted to murder him. I can still hear Doc, trying to ward a couple of them off, saying, "'Ere, leave me be, do you 'ear—leave me be." I think about the only heroic thing I have ever done in my life, outside of mixing all sorts of strange drinks, was coming to his rescue, and beating hell out of the other two kids. (*Note*: This incidentally was my last fist fight. I acted wisely in giving that business up. I would never have had a chance with Rocky Marciano, or even Mickey Rooney. In fact, I couldn't even lick Lois Andrews.) Anyway, Doc is one of the warmest and sweetest men that ever you could meet. He just wouldn't know how to hurt anybody. And I might say that he is the only one of my pals who resembles any of Ben Hecht's pals, who were all either genuises or at least had their idiosyncrasies. Doc is a philosopher, inventor, chiropodist, and bookmaker.

And so he, Sam Carlton (who wrote nearly all of my stage conversations with my mother), Desmoni, my attorney (who will have to wait a little while longer for his money), my cousin Robert Milford (which is not his right name), and my friend and manager Lew Cooper had a meeting. Lew advised me against going to Hollywood to sit at a desk. He could book me for the following season for three or four thousand dollars a week. He thought I was making a mistake.

But the rest of the boys heartily agreed with me, and so did Paul Small, my agent (who released me from my contract), when I explained that I wanted to be near my daughter so that I might get to know her and she might learn to love me—which couldn't happen if she saw me only once or twice a year.

So, on June 12, 1943, accompanied by Carlton, I came to California, rented a house in Beverly Hills, and while marking time before I was to work at the studio on July 11th, I wrote a series of articles for the New York paper *PM*. Since then *PM* has disappeared and so have most of the articles. I don't know who took them, but by some strange coincidence several of the funny lines turn up on my dear friend Eddie Cantor's TV shows! This of course is pure coincidence, even though I recall reading these articles to him in my home and he is well known for his wonderful memory.

On July 1, I was given an office and a secretary at the Fox Studios, and some scenarios to read. I didn't see Zanuck immediately and learned in a very short time that there are two Zanucks: one, outside the office, who is as gay and carefree as any young college boy, and the other in the office, who is fully concentrated on the business of making pictures from noon to the small hours of the morning and carries a whip yet, besides!

I had made up my mind that for once I would go to Hollywood with the same feeling of authority that I had on Broadway. But it didn't work out. I began to think I had made a mistake in giving up the stage. So, to keep the rod in my back straight and strong, and my ego alive, I started making speeches, telling jokes at the luncheon table, until people began to say, "Jessel is out here just to clown around. He will never produce anything."

And then one morning I read a line that the Twentieth Century-Fox New York office was thinking of making a picture based on the career of the fabulous Dolly Sisters —Rose and Jenny Dolly—who had come to America from Hungary when they were kids, and had become internationally famous as singers, dancers, actresses, favorites of dukes and earls, and had, on one occasion, broken the bank of Monte Carlo at the roulette tables.

I had known the Dolly Sisters and made up my mind that if I could produce anything, it would certainly be a story based on people of the theater. I rushed over to Zanuck's office, ad-libbed the plot, and got the assignment.

I learned in a short time—while working with writers Marian Spitzer and John Larkin—that facts have nothing to do with entertainment, and that truth, though often stranger than fiction, is completely unimportant unless it can bring laughter or tears or both. Also, the many gay things about the Dolly Sisters, their amours, etc., would not suit the requirements of the strict, silly censorship that existed in those days. I remember my last set-to with a group of censors, when they not only suggested how a scene should be changed but actually wrote it. I asked them then if they had any other business besides that of censoring and rewriting motion pictures. Because, if they did not, I advised them to find some, for within a very short time they would not have six hundred pictures a year to pass on—or even half that many—and those that would be made wouldn't survive their type of censorship that was making motion pictures fit for school children only—these same children who had ways to buy any book or borrow it from a library, or see a play, regardless of its contents, regardless of its adult level.

Movie censorship as of last year has become ever so much more adult and sensible, and the answer of course, is "that's why the movie business has been on the up-grade. [Of course, the cinnamon toast screen has helped, too.] That's why we can have great, great pictures, honestly made, like *From Here to Eternity, On the Waterfront,* and many others that could never have passed the censorship a dozen years ago." Some people believe my satirical darts like the ones in the article published in the New York *Times*—and which I am quoting below—have encouraged producers to defy the childishness of the censor boards:

"The affair at which the awards were presented was probably the most entertaining intermural festivity in Hollywood's history, the best wits in the Guild having concentrated on the preparation of the show. The most cogent comment on screen writing came from George Jessel, master of ceremonies, during the broadcast presentation of the awards. 'It is a much harder lot, writing for the screen than for the theater or the bookshelf,' Mr. Jessel said, 'for the screen writer does not have the complete canvas of life to write upon. He is held within the tight bonds of continually keeping in mind the pre-adolescent audience and the strict chains of several forms of censorship—censorship that is often wise and many, many times, unwise . . . Take for example the deservingly great success of the current New York theater: *South Pacific, Death of a Salesman, Detective Story, A Streetcar Named Desire.* With the possible exception of a few nondescript lines like 'Here he comes' or 'Tell him I'll be back soon,' I doubt whether there is one scene in any of these plays, or one long speech, that the writer would be allowed to use in a screen play. In *South Pacific* before Signor Pinza crosses a crowded room to have an enchanted evening, he tells the story of the two little children on the stage with him and their origin. We'd have to change that for the screen—those kids would turn out to be two young Annapolis midshipmen who, single-handed, lifted the battleship *Missouri* off the shoals of Chesapeake Bay . . .' "

Anyway, *The Dolly Sisters* went through that baptismal fire. I think we had to say something to the effect that they had only been kissed twice, and that by an old uncle.

Then came the casting problem. The studio wanted a vehicle for Betty Grable and Alice Faye, who would make an ideal *Dolly Sisters*, even though they were violently blonde, while the Dolly Sisters in actuality were definite brunettes. But with that I wouldn't quarrel, for outside of people in show business, nobody would hate me for two highly talented, beautiful girls who photographed so pretty in Technicolor.

Miss Faye, however, had chosen to quit the screen—and it took all the authority of Zanuck, and on my part, the diplomacy of three Pierre Mendès-Frances combined, to arrange for little June Haver—then only a starlet—to share the spotlight with the reigning favorite, Betty Grable. But it worked out well. It was good entertainment, did a tremendous business throughout the world, and Billy Wilkerson, in an editorial in the Hollywood *Reporter*, threw every orchid at me—(they grow wild on Sunset Boulevard).

After that I produced *I Wonder Who's Kissing Her Now* —based on the life and career of Joseph E. Howard (not one word of truth, but a highly entertaining picture), and another musical, *Do You Love Me*, with the song of the same name by Harry Ruby; then a drama called *Nightmare Alley*, from William Gresham's bloodcurdling story which today would have made a big hit with a fellow like Marlon Brando in the leading part of a *geek* in a carnival—and don't ask to find out what a *geek* is, you will get sick to your stomach.

This part was played, and beautifully so, by Tyrone Power, and I'll never forget the reaction of an audience in Dallas, when the picture first showed. Power played the villain in the picture and did everything that was wrong for a human being to do. The audience in Dallas, mostly kids, had never seen Ty in anything but in the part of a hero, so that when a brave young acrobat attacked Power for trying to seduce a sweet, innocent, young girl, while Power was also carrying on an affair with a married woman, the kids in the audience yelled, "Knock him down, Ty!" And then I knew my picture didn't have a chance.

I introduced in *When My Baby Smiles at Me*—a new title for the play *Burlesque*—together as a team, for the first time, Betty Grable and Dan Dailey, and in my opinion—which is anything but a humble one—these two gave the best performances of their entire careers, and the public agreed with me.

Among many others of my productions, one close to my heart was *Wait 'til the Sun Shines, Nellie*, in which a performance that I've never seen bettered was given by David Wayne, whose great talent wouldn't be recognized by critics until after he scored on Broadway in *The Teahouse of the August Moon.*

Another picture was an expensive attempt to bring high-class music, ballet, and opera to the screen, called *Tonight We Sing*, based on the career of Hurok, the impresario, with Wayne as Hurok, Pinza as Chaliapin, Tamara Toumanova as Pavlova, Roberta Peters, Jan Peerce, and many other world-famous artists. Maybe Cinemascope would have saved this, but Cinemascope had not arrived yet, and this picture was successful only in Europe and nowhere else, according to General Box Office.

Outside of bringing little Miss Haver to the fore, my favorite discovery is Mitzi Gaynor, who is just chockful of talent, and if I ever again produce a motion picture, I would like to do the life of Fannie Brice with Mitzi as Fannie. But I've been told lately by an agent for the story that the character would have to be a combination of Barbara Fritchie and Sister Kenny and I couldn't produce it that way and heaven knows Fannie wouldn't want it that way either.

I would say that my ten years at Twentieth Century-Fox are easily the most fruitful of my long career, surely the happiest, for outside of producing many pictures, the security of a long contract gave me a clarity of mind and allowed me to use many resources that had never been tapped before. I have been able to be active in many charitable and benevolent organizations; I spoke on two occasions to a group of men and raised the money to build two houses of worship; I created the Friars' Club of California, which has done more good for those less fortunate than all of the other theatrical clubs all over the world put together. We arranged one performance at the Shrine Auditorium in Los Angeles, in which the Friars were able to give a check to the Motion Picture Relief Fund for over three hundred thousand dollars. Being a producer has made me the recipient of more New Year's greetings in one year than I received in a lifetime and has brought to my office some beautiful girls.

But the one thing that stands out in the Zanuck decade, and the most important event, is when I acted as public relations liaison for a splendid motion picture, entitled *Wilson*, actually based on the life of the great Democratic president. This picture didn't make any money but did an awful lot of good, and the picture business was in such a fine shape then (before TV) that it was worth while to make such a picture, as what it might lose would be brought in by a few extra Westerns.

Zanuck gave his heart and soul and mind to this picture

(despite the fact he is an ardent Republican), and we went together to the White House to show it to President Roosevelt, his family, and a small group. When the picture was over Zanuck was lionized. Although Mr. Roosevelt could smile sometimes and not always mean it, he certainly did after seeing *Wilson*. I can see him now, in his chair, with his arm around Darryl, and hear him say: "Colonel, what has Georgie Jessel got to do with this?" And with an apology I interrupted and said, "Mr. President, I have been very anxious about the picture and feel it is for the good of the world that the people see it—and not only that, but I have ambitions for Mr. Zanuck. If he sets his mind to it, some day he, too, may be president—and then, I'll be the Jewish Jim Farley."

Among the special group which had been invited to see the picture was a little retiring man in a Palm Beach suit, whom I had met some years ago in Kansas City. We got to talking, and he said, "I thought the picture was wonderful. I wanted to tell Mr. Zanuck so, but I think he feels that I don't like him." I asked why. He replied: "Well, he thinks I slighted him in some Army report." I said, "Oh, I don't think so—" and then I went over to Darryl and said, "I think you ought to straighten this out, because you are a swell fellow, and so is—" and I pointed. So, I brought Zanuck over. I said, "Darryl, you know Senator Harry Truman?" and they shook hands.

I had ten consecutive years in the movies. My productions made money, the hits outnumbering the failures. I was able to acquire the friendships of two presidents, and I am so proud of this because even though my dear friend Cantor knew General Grant and Jefferson Davis, he never was on such intimate terms as I have been with Roosevelt and Truman.

Jeri, should you wish to go into show business when you are say, around seventeen, I'll have you do your stuff for some of my pals, like Benny, Cantor, Burns and Hope, and if they agree with me that you have talent, I will insist that you concentrate on the amusement business and go into it with everything you've got—as an actress or as a writer. And with the experience you will already have had in a few TV and theater appearances, you will have a much better chance than the pretty little misses who enter the movies like, for example, the young lady in the following pages.

5. Beauty and Busts

Despite the fact that less movies are being made than ever before, the urge to be a screen star has not diminished accordingly, and once in a great while a Grace Kelly becomes a star practically overnight.

You can watch the International Airport at Inglewood or the railroad station at Los Angeles, and you are sure to see a new group of young girls bent on a career in the movies. The fact that Miss Kelly is a highly educated, cultured young lady, who has been studying for years to be an actress, does not stop these other little damsels who have so little of these requisites, except that they are pretty. What happens to most of them, I think, can best be told in the following observation:

My friend, Ben Hecht, novelist extraordinaire, has recently written some rather violent things against motion picturedom, the locale of its most important origin, and about the general morals of the people who serve it. Why he has chosen to do this, I don't know. Maybe it is good showmanship. Maybe this one particular chapter of the low-thinking, below-the-belt life in Hollywood as he sees it will help the sale of his book, although the rest of his autobiography surmounts this particular chapter by at least five or six hundred pages of wonderful memories.

It is strange that Ben has always had this attitude about Hollywood, in spite of the fact that it has admired and respected him so much and has shown its admiration in the most practical way possible, with currency of the realm. Also, to my knowledge, it never insisted that he prostitute his pen, and some of his writing for the screen has been of the same high caliber as his early novels, like *Eric Dorn,* as well as his present tome, *A Child of the Century.*

Hecht's attitude about the movies has always reminded me of a gay young man I met who came to Palm Beach in the halcyon days and always talked about how he hated the idea of having to make love to an old woman just to get money. Actually he never had to do that. The gals he had were always young and beautiful. But for some reason it was always, "I guess I'll have to find another old bag again next winter."

I never could account for that, any more than I can account for the delightful night-club comic, Joe E. Lewis, insisting upon telling audiences that he is always violently tipsy and is dead-broke because he loses every dollar gambling, while actually he is pretty sober, has quite a bit of money in annuities kept for him by the well-known Judge A. L. Marovitz in Chicago, and Joe always has wonderfully entertaining material that is in no way dependent upon the premise of being stewed or without the next meal.

After having been in and out of the picture business from 1926 to 1942, and in it completely from 1942 to 1952, I feel that I can speak and write very clearly about the movies and its people. And in my experience I have found that Hollywood has not hurt the people who have to write for a living, but mostly the ones who have to go wrong for a living.

Take little Mabel Zunza. She is the most sought-after gal at Crovney High School in Crovney, U.S.A. Crovney is near some larger city in which there is a movie theater which is part of the largest chain in the state. So it becomes worth while to incorporate a newsreel shot of Crovney's annual girls' basketball game or some such healthy gimmick. So Mabel Zunza gets in a newsreel, and she looks pretty good.

From this either a couple of local gentlemen foresee a career for her or maybe the newsreel cameraman himself (a little on the make) tells somebody and somebody sends for a few feet of film, and then maybe in some sort of beauty contest Mabel Zunza is entered and wins the prize, which is a trip to Hollywood, a test at a movie studio, expenses paid for Mabel and Mother, or most times, Mabel and Mother's sister, a kindly auntie who is not behind the times. She can smoke a cigarette and drink a coke and bourbon and still go to church on Sunday. She cries easily at every movie, because everything reminds her of her husband Charlie who left the world too soon.

There's a big to-do in Crovney. A party, a lacrimose love scene with Mabel and the kid who's stuck on her. He's had cokes and bourbon a couple more times than he's ever had before and therefore speaks his feelings with all the bars down. Mabel might as well know the truth, he wishes she hadn't won the contest, for he knows now he'll never see her again. She'll probably run away with Tony Curtis or George Raft, and his is a broken life. And then Mabel, with the voice she thinks is a combination of Deborah Kerr, Elizabeth Taylor, and Anne Baxter, tells him she'll never forget him. She won't stay in Hollywood no matter what they offer her, and all the dreams they had will come true. She'll be back and they'll continue to go out every night, and she'll write him every day—and with one hand she lifts up his chin and says, "You believe me, don't you?"—and with the other hand she tightly squeezes the railroad ticket to the Coast, which auntie, a little bit *shikker*, has left in the john.

A hundred good-byes, the high school band at the railroad station—"Good-by, everybody." "Good-by, Mabel." "Tell Gregory Peck he can put his shoes under my bed." "Be sure and kiss Joan Crawford for me." "Send us a picture in your red Jaguar." "Good-by, everybody."

A few tears shed by the family, and rightly so, and off goes Mabel Zunza, avec duenna, en route to Baghdad-on-Close-up.

The picture company fulfills its every promise. A press agent and a photographer are at the Union Station in Los Angeles, or even more stylish, in Pasadena. Mabel gets her picture took. Auntie gets in a couple (these will never be printed). She's taken to a good hotel. She'll be there at least a week, maybe more, depending upon how long it will take to make a photographic test, and if it turns out well, there will be a dialogue test to follow and perhaps a stock contract for at least six months at about seventy-five dollars a week, which will not be enough for Mabel and auntie to continue to live at the hotel. For only this week's room and vittles will be paid for by the company and then Mabel will be on her own.

The next day to the studio and probably a quick hand-

shake with the boss, and maybe a director who's just finished a conference, and then to one or two of the sets with
introductions to a prominent star or two, and Mabel Zunza
is in her eighth heaven.

Did auntie notice how Rock Hudson looked at her—to
which auntie answers, "No, honey, I didn't. I was too excited
looking at the man who was arranging those flowers. I don't
see why he isn't acting. He's handsome."

I hope I haven't been facetious in making it seem like
this lovely little Mabel and her aunt are just schmoes. They
are not. They are very nice people who have gotten into a
game that is a million-to-one shot against them. And the
fact that they come from a small town doesn't make any
difference, because no matter who you are—if it's a little
girl in a stock company from Umglick, Massachusetts or a
kid from New York who's been seen in a school play—when
they reach the stage of making a movie test in Hollywood,
what happens after that goes for everybody. Poor little baby
peacocks—one may soon boast of beautifully colored feath-
ers, most will soon be plucked of their tiny plumage.

For every Lana Turner and Ava Gardner there are thousands whose last appearance on the screen is that first photographic test.

Mabel's test is made in time, during that one week when
the company pays the hotel bill. However, it may be some
time before the test is shown to the executive members of
the film company, because so-and-so is out of town or so-
and-so is on location or so-and-so can only be found at Santa
Anita. Mabel is advised that it would be smart if she went
back home and if her test is good they will contact her and
she can return, if and when they want her to do anything
further.

But Mabel talks it over with auntie. Isn't it silly to go

home; it may be only a few days or a few hours before the test is seen by a big shot. It is so decided. They'll stay, but not at the hotel. They'll move to a smaller place—that lovely little motel behind Chasen's Restaurant. Harry, Mabel's dad, will understand and, if necessary, send them the money required.

Now a few days later Mabel is notified that the test is pretty good. She can look at it herself. Some of the directors have seen it and she should report at the studio the following morning. I haven't the energy that it would take to write of the enthusiasm and the high hopes that are rushing through Mabel and auntie. All sorts of day and night dreams of the rosiest future and what members of the family will be brought to Hollywood first, and what to tell the kid back home who has written a half-dozen letters daily. What about Susan's face, the girl next door who had been heard to whisper, "I don't see what Mabel's got." Well, she'll see, won't she, Auntie?

The following morning they see the test. Mabel looks pretty good. In fact, the studio camera and with real good makeup is certainly pounds the best over the film in the newsreel taken at Crovney Stadium, and the studio decides to put Mabel under a contract for six months. During that time there will be a dialogue test.

She gets a six months' contract at seventy-five a week, with options for seven years. She'll be an extra in the meantime or do tiny bits, etc. Now comes the first of the letters home. To the girls at school: "Well, kids, I made it!" To the boy: "No matter how big a star I am it won't make any difference. Don't be upset if you don't hear from me as often as you have been writing me, but there's so much to do and also a couple of previews I must go to. It's a studio order."

Now Mabel Zunza has to have a new name. The studio

hasn't decided what it will be, but it won't be Mabel Zunza. It will be something like Mora Zane, or Mara Kane—now, let's settle for Melba Cross.

By this time living in a motel is a little awkward. First of all there's no phone. They've got to run to the front office. So maybe it would be best if auntie went home until after the dialogue test, for of course there'll be a new long contract. Then auntie can come back and they'll have a maid and an apartment. And so, auntie goes back, leaving behind her Mabel Zunza, who, it seems like only yesterday, used to fall asleep in auntie's arms, and now she is Melba Cross, a starlet in the movies with her own motel room and, before you know it, an automobile.

Now for some reason or other, the studio decides to cut down on its dialogue tests; unless something comes along that is "just dynamite" there's no need to spend this money. Well, little Melba Cross isn't "just dynamite." She's a nice little girl with a cute little kisser, and they're a dime a dozen. Lanas and Avas are hard to find.

Besides the reports from the studio acting school headed by Madame Tchickeznic, who was formerly with the Stanislovski Company (as a second wardrobe mistress), are that Melba will need so much work—oh, so much work. And so there is no dialogue test, and about a month before the six months' contract is ended a nice guy around the studio who's been taking Melba to Schwab's drugstore and a drive-in, slips her the news that he's heard they won't pick up her option. And they don't.

This is done very gently. She's told if a part comes up, they'll certainly send for her. And the nice guy from the studio is not a fellow on the make. He's got a gal on location with a picture. Melba's nice company, and he advises her that maybe she ought to go home and wait there for the good news, instead of going into hock by staying in Hollywood.

Now this is quite a blow to Melba. She doesn't know just how to write this news back home. But, as she stands at the motel window with eyes filled up, the phone rings. It's one of the other little optionets at the studio. This young lady is getting some of the girls together for a party that a producer is giving to celebrate a finished picture, made a couple of days under schedule. Melba goes to the party. Most of the people know each other very well, and if anyone attending has any inhibitions, it's only Melba, who is still like she was when she left Crovney as of eight o'clock, Pacific Standard Time. She goes to the party and everybody gets a little high very early, because this party has started on the set at the studio, so that by ten o'clock many people have shown up that were not even invited or that saw cars outside and just stepped in to get a fast drink before they are asked who they are.

In the johnny three of the little dolls are huddling, two advising Melba. The studio would have never dropped her if she'd gotten in to see the big boss, D.L. He likes girls with hair like Melba's and he would have certainly used his influence. That's a little late now, so what she ought to do is go out and make a little fuss over Jed Strauss, the press agent who dropped in. He can get her into the columns because most of his clients are night clubs and restaurants. He can print that she's been out with George Raft, Georgie Jessel, or any available bachelor, regardless of the vintage. That's the thing to do. Then somebody will take notice of her.

Melba meets the P.A. As a matter of fact, they leave the party a little bit ahead of the others, have a nightcap, and he takes her home. He leaves her with a much more experienced pair of lips than she had at home, and certainly he'll help her. He'll take her out himself to a place that sometimes is frequented by Johnny Kane who knows a fellow who knows Howard Hughes—and who knows what can happen?

It is now four-forty in the morning, but Melba is too excited to hit the hay. This is the time to write another letter home, and it won't hurt to tell a little lie, because it's all going to work out well. And so the content of the letter is something like this: "I have left the studio because I would just be wasting my time. All they care about is Lana and Ava and I would never get anywhere at that studio, unless, of course, I would have gone out with a certain director and gone to his apartment which, of course, you know I wouldn't do."

So Melba goes out with the press agent and gets her name in a couple of columns: "that pretty girl at Mocambo last night dancing with the well-known TV comedian is Melba Cross, who they say just made a hot test at Metro." Or maybe she may even get a box in Harrison Carroll's column, like: "What producer having dinner at the Luau last night was holding Melba Cross's hand?"

But all this doesn't help Melba as far as her career is concerned, because Melba is just a pretty little girl. They're a dime a dozen. Melba is not "just dynamite." Those girls are two in a million, like Lana and Ava.

And now she's broke. She's written a couple of more letters with some good lies that more experienced girls have helped her with, like: "I was up for a very big part, but I just couldn't stand the advances of the casting director, and they're all that way at nearly all the studios. I expect to play a part in one of the little theaters where all the talent scouts come, and I'm sure that's going to lead to something. Thanks for the fifty dollars. I'll pay it back ten times before you know it."

That letter's to auntie. Then there's another letter in answer to the boy back home who has seen one of the squibs in a syndicated column or in a movie magazine. He's made up his mind to come out to California. Melba, of course, tells him he must not do this. He must wait until she's playing a star part, and he is not to believe what he reads in the columns. She goes out very little, even though he'd be surprised at the big stars who have invited her, etc.

Around about this time Melba has made up her mind that maybe the best way to get anywhere is to go anywhere and not be impossible to make. And before you know it, Melba makes the rounds, and the rounds make Melba. But regardless of the circumstances, nothing seems to be as bad as going home to Crovney and admitting, "I failed in Hollywood." So, like most Melbas, formerly Mabels, she stays on and hooks up with a fellow and goes steady. He takes care of her eating for a while, but that's about as serious as he is; and when that's over, Melba has to find some kind of a job or be on the town. But any job suffers so by comparison with the dreams of even being a small-part actress that Melba couldn't think of taking a job in a store, except a little modeling. But Melba is not quite tall enough for evening stuff.

Now by this time a year or so has passed. There's no chance of Melba going home now. There are too many things she'd have to lie about, and besides there is a young actor she's quite fond of, a young ham with whom she's able to get off all the acting steam which she had no other opportunity to do. They read scripts together. Besides he may have a future, and so comes the next letter home: "I have met so-and-so and he wants to marry me, but he says I must give up acting, and he's so right, because you can't have a home and a career as well. I'll tell you all about it in a few weeks as soon as he gets his new contract."

Now, sometimes the promising young ham does marry the little girl who misses, but not very often. The girls who miss are a dime a dozen. They're not all Lanas and Avas. They're not "just dynamite."

So Melba Cross gets the air and finally takes up with an older man who keeps her, sees her once in a while. But because it's only once in a while, he keeps her only fairly well.

By this time Melba has learned to drink pretty vigorously. Also Melba can't sleep, so Melba takes a sleeping pill, and after a while one doesn't work so Melba takes two or three, which find her awfully groggy in the morning, so she takes a little vodka to wake her up, and:

> "The time has come," the doctor said,
> "To talk of many ills,
>   Of Hollywood and saddish girls
>   And schnapps and sleeping pills."

And so it goes. As long as Melba can keep fairly good-looking and be most accommodating, it will continue for a few years, and Melba will wake up every morning sorry about the night before, then not give a damn, and take all the pills or climb a tree in a car.

Now you can't blame Hollywood for this. The movie magazines, the press agents, the personal appearances have been painted in such glamorous colors that the tiniest moth leaps at any possible opportunity for a try at the flame. Some are singed, but most are burned. Oh, so few succeed. The rest are a dime a dozen. They're not like Lana and Ava, Marilyn or Gina Lollobrigida. A few have dynamite, most have busts.

*Honey, the year you were born, 1941, radio was
at its highest peak. Amos and Andy was a must, as was
Jack Benny, the Lux Show, Fred Allen, Ben Bernie;
and Fibber McGee and Molly, Eddie Cantor, and Kate
Smith were in complete charge of the public ear.*

*Since then, TV has completely taken over the ear,
because of the eye. And today radio has to depend on
the people who are driving their cars and the house
ladies in the morning who, not being able to do their
chores while gazing at TV, have to be content to listen
to the little radio in the kitchen.*

*In fact, at this moment, I am preparing to do a
Breakfast Show for radio. They are easy to do, as the
audience does most of the work. I doubt that I'll do
more than four or five TV "guest shows" during the
year.*

*However, TV is a wonderful thing. General Sarnoff
and Manie Sacks, of NBC, showed me the latest color
show the other day, and it was breath-taking.*

*And since I have been quoted in the magazines and
columns on this subject, I thought I'd write you a piece
on it, in which I throw orchids at some and brickbats
at others.*

6. TV—and Some Inmates of it

GODFREY, CROSBY, WINCHELL

FOR WHAT PURPOSE TV? Like many new art
forms, the business of TV suffers from the fact that it wan-
ders off in all directions. When I use the word "suffer," I
mean that only for the people who work in it, certainly not
for audiences, as they get the best of it, for they can sit home

with or without clothes, do anything they like while the show is on, and the price is right.

But most of the people who work in TV find that there is a great lack of coordination. Last year I was sponsored by four products and entered the television business with this set idea: to sell the products that were paying me, for I believed that was what I was supposed to do. When the sponsor asked me to deliver the commercial personally, I did it. When the sponsor told me to take out some dialogue or a song to make room for the commercial, I did it. I had no other interference as far as entertainment was concerned, for my clients believed that I should know something about that part of it, having acted, produced, and spoken publicly for more than forty years, rather successfully.

The average TV show doesn't have that kind of mutual cooperation. The sponsor's idea is the same: to sell his wares by way of drawing attention to his product; and in ever so many cases the sponsors use TV for what they call "institutional advertising," this refers to products that actually don't need selling, but still must always be kept under the eye, the argument being that when "Sapolio" stopped talking about itself, and "Uneeda Biscuits" discontinued their three-sheets of the little boy in the raincoat, it was the end of them. And then, of course, there are companies which say: "We might as well spend the extra money or we will have to give it to the government anyway . . ."

But most of the actors constantly worry about the criticisms of their close friends who watch them weekly. This brings intimacy to such a high point that people who like you personally and are close to you find it hard to laugh at your jokes every week and are bound to find fault with you. Then the producer and the director worry about the weekly press, for every show is an opening night, and most of the critics treat a TV show in the same manner as they do a play, forgetting completely that there is actually about two days of rehearsal and four days of writing for each half-hour show, whereas the average playwright may take two years to write his play, then rewrite it for six months, then rehearse it for more than a month. TV and radio and, more particularly, motion pictures, have been hurt by the press who for years has been taking the average picture apart, expecting to find the same kind of entertainment, created for the four-dollar literate theatergoer, presented for the average motion picture price of about seventy-five cents. And on TV and radio the public gets it for nothing. The advertising agencies have only one idea in mind: the ratings and the surveys.

In more than forty years as a public entertainer, serving in practically every capacity except in the circus and burlesque, I have never known anything as inaccurate or completely cockeyed as those so-called popularity polls. These are based on a few phone calls in a few cities, never taking into consideration that there are thousands of people who can well afford to buy any product advertised and who, for one reason or another, have unlisted telephones. Thus, their opinions of what they like or dislike or listen to don't seem to count. In addition, there are people like my own particular little audience (if I may be so bold) who live in hotels and apartments that have switchboards and no personal telephone numbers. There are at least a few million of these, and their preference also does not seem to count.

The number of phone calls made by these pulse-takers is ridiculously small. They ring up a few people and then multiply their answers by something like 1,378,311. The result, they have you believe, reflects the popularity of TV shows throughout the country, and what America is looking at on every sponsored hour.

This is as if I were to ask three guys in New York's garment center what they had for lunch that day. If two of them should answer, "We had chopped liver and onions," the survey would then prove that two men out of three in the U.S. eat chopped liver and onions for lunch.

My first sponsor last year was a pen company which, before my going on TV, was practically unknown east of the Mississippi. After a few shows the pen started to sell like wildfire all over the country. Most of my shows came through on a TV set on what is called Kinescope. This means that despite the fact that they are made live, and not on film, the majority of stations use them on Kinescope film, sometimes two weeks after they are actually performed. Therefore, the first surveys, particularly the Trendex, never seemed to find anybody at home to answer the phone about me. Incidentally, Trendex makes calls in only ten cities. The great cities like St. Louis and Kansas City in the Middle West are never called. Pittsburgh and other great communities that have tremendous buying power get no phone calls at all. And, of course, neither do the hundreds of other prosperous hamlets throughout the country.

But somebody must have been watching my show, or how would they have heard of the pen, and what would have urged them to ask for it in local stores?

I was able to discover very definitely that people were watching my show, because on a speaking tour of seventy days in seventy different cities, people would wait for me at the airport, kids would recognize me on the street and ask when my daughter Jerilynn was going to go on again and when I was going to talk to my mother on the telephone. They certainly could not have been people who had seen me on Broadway in *The Jazz Singer* thirty years ago!

To show to what absurd degree this rating business can

go, the following story is the absolute truth: Some years ago I was engaged to do a weekly program, a commentary. The product was a beer called VX. The money was put up by the beer company, given to an agency, the agency bought the time and my services for thirteen weeks and I went on, but the beer was never made. Not one bottle was ever brewed. I went on every week and there were long arguments about the commercial. One day the agency almost came to blows over the following: "Why say: *go* to your nearest tavern for VX beer? Change it to: *run* to your nearest tavern." Another day, there was almost blood spilled over this: "Why should we say: this is as good as any Canadian ale?—It's better!" We then added to the commercial that people should send in bottle tops and they would win a prize. All this for a product that was nonexistent, but the rating was good and to this day that particular advertising agency is patting itself on the back for the great job it did.

Advertising agencies, from the most important to the smallest, swear by Trendex and similar surveys, and, because of these ratings obtained by making a few scattered phone calls, they are never on the spot when they have to give their personal opinion as to whether a show is good or bad or whether the artist has any talent. Therefore they can never be told by the sponsor: "You booked this girl, or you chose this type of show . . ." For no matter what the reaction is from the audience that sees it actually performed, no matter how they might scream with laughter, cry at a sentimental scene, or be captured by the suspense of a show —this has nothing to do with it. The fate of the show and its artists and its creators is always dependent on that point up and down in the ratings, like a poor gambler on the stock market with a margin account to whom every eighth up and down is a benediction.

Last year at a performance of the Metropolitan Opera House of *The Barber of Seville,* beautifully sung and acted by Merrill, Peters, Siepi, and others, I was sitting next to a prominent TV advertising executive. The audience cheered and rose to its feet at the final curtain. Even the most reticent cried, "Bravo, bravo . . ." The advertising man never moved a muscle—no doubt forgetting he was in a theater and thinking that he could venture no approval or disapproval of the performance until there were some phone calls made.

I got another advertising man off his guard one day as we walked along Fifth Avenue. I said to him, "Isn't that a pretty girl over there?" He replied, "I won't know until the ratings are in."

The incident that caused me to speak my mind about this business happened at a time when I was not in the TV business and could have no possible ax to grind. I was asked to appear on a very big revue program, but being under contract to Twentieth Century-Fox, which prohibited TV appearances, I was not available for it. In my place they engaged an act of well-known comedians—the comedians created laughter more by gesture and grimace than they did with words or thoughts. These fellows had a wonderful act in night clubs and were a riot in vaudeville. They brought their own tried and true material to the TV producer and explained to him that where they had just one page of dialogue, this particular bit would run four or five minutes, as the audience screamed. Another bit which on paper would last but a few lines was again a hilarious piece of business, which ran another four or five minutes, because of the continued laughter of the audience. So, the show went on—but it was televised from a tremendous studio, quite far away from where there is any civilization, and it is hard to get audiences to come out there. Sometimes the network has to bring them by bus from the city, and those that do come are not what we call "hep" audiences, or they would not be available at four or five o'clock on a Saturday or Sunday afternoon to ride for a couple of hours just to see forty minutes of entertainment and hear twenty minutes of commercials. These audiences consist of women and kids who have nothing better to do, sometimes people from the smaller towns of California, tourists in Hollywood who are happy to be taken out for some little entertainment. And so, the show went on . . . the comics did their bits exactly as they do them for more sophisticated and paying audiences, but under the circumstances of playing to a hick audience, and four big cameras blotting out the view of most of them, the laughter was missing, and the bit that generally ran five minutes ran a minute and a half. There was no waiting for laughs. When they came to the end of the show, the producer frantically found himself five minutes short, and there was pandemonium at the studio.

Now, of course, with a Berle, a Hope, a Cantor, or a Benny, these five minutes could easily be filled with anecdotes or even an explanation of why the show was short—and getting some fun out of it for all concerned with impromptu remarks. But as I have told you, the comics in the show were not monologists, or ad-lib speakers. They tried to fill out the five minutes as best they could, and finally they spied an old gentleman in the audience, with a completely bald head. They found a bowl of sugar on the prop table, had the camera focused on the bald old gentleman, poured a little sugar on his head, stuck their tongues out, and started licking the old man's head for at least three minutes to fill out the time. This became not only violently unpleasant to the people watching but nauseating even to the people who had been brought there for nothing and had been given candy bars to munch on. Even a hungry cannibal couldn't stand seeing a bald-headed man getting his head licked for that length of time and enjoy it.

Anyhow, the show was finally over. The following morning everybody concerned waited for the reports as if waiting for the electric chair. The man acting for the client of the advertising agency was named Tiny or Small or some such name—it does not come to me at the moment. He, of course, had not seen the show, but the Trendex had gone up one eighth, and his wire to those concerned was as follows: *Did not see show but Trendex up. Engage boys again to repeat the performance.*

The boys, of course, would do no such thing.

Now, read this carefully, if you please, for the sake of what your children might have to look at. Had these comics accepted the engagement, and the Trendex gone up another one eighth, this ad man would have no doubt engaged the boys for a long series, and the American people might have turned on their TV sets weekly and have seen the disgusting sight of a couple of middle-aged men licking the head of a bald man at the end of each performance. (*Note:* These comics are no longer in the amusement business—one owns a sugar plantation in Cuba, the other is a very successful building contractor in Maine.)

Only lately I made thirty telephone calls throughout Greater New York, and this is what happened:

I took a number at random from a phone book and said: "I am speaking for the Praldo Company. We are a TV survey company. Do you have a TV?"
A.—Of course we do. We were the first ones on our street to have one. Everybody used to come to our house until

Mrs. Phelps got hers, and then of course—(this is a very talkative dame).

Q.—Thank you, and which channel do you generally tune in to?

A.—Channel two—NBC.

Q.—And do you tune in on Thursdays?

A.—Of course. That's the night my husband stays home. He generally plays cards on Friday and Saturday, etc.

Q.—What show do you watch particularly on Thursday night on NBC?

A.—Oh, the Jackie Gleason show—we never miss it . . .

Q.—Thank you, madam.

Now, the Jackie Gleason show is on CBS on Saturday night! Seven out of ten answers were as inaccurate as this, and the last two answers, when I asked what their favorite TV shows were, were as follows: From a lady in the Bronx: "The show I prefer is Georgie Jessel's 'This Is Your Life'— but my husband likes 'Duffy's Tavern!'" Now, of course, I am sure you know that "This Is Your Life" is a Ralph Edwards show, and not mine, and at the time I made these calls, "Duffy's Tavern" had not yet appeared on TV.

Another thing that minds have to be made up about is the fact that TV is not the theater or motion picture and is not related to these other forms in any way, and I think that this is a fact that must definitely be saluted because the greatest success on TV is Arthur Godfrey who, I understand, has only been on the stage once, and I am told on good authority that he very seldom goes to the theater.

To sum it up, my solution is to watch the cash register. If they are buying the stuff, they are watching you. That's how the story is told, with cash on the counter and not the

fluctuating up a point or down a point in the so-called ratings.

And most important of all, the American is the most individualistic fellow in the world. His opinion, like himself,
cannot be regimented. That is what makes him different. If
you ask the average Englishman what he will be doing between four and five in the afternoon, he will tell you he is
having tea, and you can multiply that several million times
and be correct. If you ask the average Frenchman what he
is doing at that time, he will lift an eyebrow at you. But you
can walk into any hotel in America and quiz three elevator
boys about anything, and about the only thing they will
agree on probably is Marilyn Monroe.

The next awful thing about TV and the radio business is
the fact that the artist is not paid until ten days, sometimes
two weeks, after he has finished his work. Of course this is
all right for the big fellows who are under contract at thousands of dollars weekly, so ten days' or two weeks' delay
does not mean anything. But there are hundreds of little
fellows, actors and actresses, many of whom have been important in the theater and now, perforce of circumstances,
have to do the best they can, and jump at the opportunity
of saying a line or two on a TV or radio show, for just
enough money to pay room rent. They've got to wait ten
days or two weeks before they get those few dollars. I have
known many actors, around Christmas time, who played
some tiny bit in a TV skit or radio just to be able to bring
something home for the kids, but they aren't paid until after
the New Year.

There is an organization called AFRA that represents TV
and radio artists. Just how it functions, or what aid it is, I
haven't yet been told. I do know that I've been fighting and
pleading with them to do something to see that this wrong is

corrected. In answer to my letters and speeches, they told me that this is a procedure that has always existed; the advertising companies never pay until after ten days, because of —etc., etc. And I answer: This procedure will have to be changed, because it was also a procedure for men to rub flint together in order to make a fire; this changed. It was also a procedure for King George III to put such a heavy tax on tea—then one early morning, they found the tea at the bottom of Boston Harbor. Only a few years ago, when my Uncle Morris walked on the streets of Berlin, it was also a procedure for the Nazis to shoot him. All procedures that are unfair are eventually changed, and so it will be someday on TV and radio. When a man finishes his work, he will be paid. He will not have to wait until golf games and martini parties are over and checks go through several people before he can eat.

Of the most important personalities on TV and radio, there are a few whose listening or watching audiences are legion, and this is borne out by the fact that whatever they have advertised, they have sold in tremendous quantities.

Tops has been Arthur Godfrey. I heard it said that somebody can come to him in the morning with a new breakfast food—Doodle Wheat or Lecky Flakes—or any other name that has just been coined the night before—and as Godfrey goes off the air, the grocery shops are stampeded with orders for it. I don't know Mr. Godfrey very well. I met him once or twice at the Stork Club and once at the Kentucky Derby, and you cannot learn much about a man under such gay and happy circumstances, particularly at the Kentucky Derby, where everybody is everybody's dear old pal. On Derby Day if you ask a stranger what time it is, he gives you his watch as a present. The manners, and even the dialect, of the "Ole South" become the order of the day, and people from the garment center of New York imagine they are "Amos and Andy." And right before the big race, when the old band in the minstrel parade uniforms plays "My Old Kentucky Home," you see people wiping tears from their eyes—people who not only were not born in Kentucky, had never been in Kentucky, but have only just tasted a *Minsk* julep for the first time.

But even under these happy circumstances, made even happier by sitting in Bill Corum's office—he is the head man of the Kentucky Derby—it seemed hard to get any slant on Arthur Godfrey's inner personality. However, despite the many things that have been said "agin" him by some people, I am inclined to think that this is really the usual thing that happens in the lives of very successful men. I cannot believe that as worldly a fellow as Godfrey would rule over his dynasty of young actors and actresses and help in general like Ivan the Terrible; and it is hard for me to believe that he has pronounced his hatred for all the members of the tribe of Moses, Jesus, and Isaiah, even though they be re- moved from them by thousands of years, like myself and William S. Paley. I just think there are a lot of people jealous of good old Arthur . . .

And as far as his having purchased an interest in a hotel which discriminates against people of the older religion, it is hard to believe that, too. I own a few shares in several companies, and how do I know how they feel about the rise of the Goldbergs?

The artist who has survived longest in radio and could also in TV if he wished it, is the highly talented fellow, Bing Crosby. This is truly a man who has found the amusement business to be his oyster. A naturally great actor, or better still, a great natural actor—creator of a style of singing, blessed with a higher intelligence than the contrived speeches on radio like, "and now we give out with, etc., etc."

Crosby, too, is a hard man to know. I met him in the days of his early beginnings in the show business. We played in sketches together at the Paramount Theatre in New York. I was one of the first fellows around Broadway to scream his praises in the Friars' Club, and all along the Rialto. And then suddenly he withdrew from the gang—like a fellow who has gone broke and doesn't want to see his intimates any more, or like a fellow who has been afflicted with something that he will only allow his mirror to see.

It was through him that I started the Friars' Club in California. We took the picture which you will find in this book, and in eight years I don't believe he has ever put his head in the door—at least, I've never seen him. He has refused to come to or appear at any of our dinners or shows for the less fortunate; he wouldn't even take a seat alongside of Bob Hope at a dinner given right in town for Bob—and the proceeds of which went to a worthy cause. And we were told that he was around the corner dining with some ball-players. Maybe he has good reasons to duck a lot of fellows who would like to love him dearly, like me. I wish he'd tell me. It would seem so simple for him to be like George M. Cohan: great with the public and great with the gang.

Another dynamic personality on TV and radio is the columnist Walter Winchell. We were singing partners in 1910. In the last dozen years I've seen him but little. My name very seldom appears in his column, regardless of the many hundreds of dinners I have spoken at, and from which my remarks have been quoted by most of the columnists in America, as well as in London, Paris, and Rome.

I believe the last squib in a Winchell column about me was: "G. Jessel in late spots with Fritzi Regan . . ." (a young lady whom I've never met, but whose steady fellow threatened to choke me, holding my neck with one hand and Winchell's column with the other).

Only a short time ago the Friars' Club of California tendered a dinner to him in appreciation of the great work he has done for the Runyon Cancer Fund. I was asked to be the toastmaster and was reluctant to take the assignment. It seemed rather awkward, under the circumstances, to affectionately introduce a man at a dinner who evidently has so little regard for me and is so pally with some others who have voiced their displeasure at practically everything I've done—maybe for the reason that these few chaps had been edited by me or chastised by me at the speaker's table. They are clever fellows too; but speech-making is the least of their talents, which they refuse to recognize. They are not satisfied with their great success in other forms of show business —which, incidentally, brings them more popularity and more currency of the realm in one month than I have ever earned in two decades of dinner-speaking. But, anyway, the Committee of the Friars told me that Walter had accepted the dinner, in which they had promised me as toastmaster; and some of my intimates said, "If he doesn't like you now, it certainly won't help much to refuse to speak at his dinner!"

And so we all came to the Beverly Wilshire Hotel ballroom—all men—had the customary nips before we sat down, and an old pal of Winchell's, a man with whom we had once sung as The Imperial Trio, Jack Wiener, came in. We took pictures together, and the evening began. The speeches were eloquent and very funny—the stag audience giving a latitude

for language that none but the Friars use . . . Jack Benny,
George Burns, Pat O'Brien, the eminent barrister Jerry Gies-
ler and David Tannenbaum, the mayor of Beverly Hills,
were among the speakers.

I had had a lot of fun with them, kidding them all sar-
castically, as per custom, and now it came to the guest of
honor. Since this is one of the few speeches which I did not
prepare on paper, this is in substance what I said:

". . . and now, gentlemen, it becomes my function to present to you the guest of honor, whose valiant efforts in the
fight against cancer have deserved our salutations and the
lifting of our glasses. I have known Walter for forty-five
years. We have not been close friends all this time, but I've
known him for forty-five years. We disagree on many things.
For example, despite the fact that you have heard most humorous talks tonight by Benny and Burns and O'Brien and
others, don't be surprised if in Walter's next column, you
read of this dinner that Milton Berle came in with his front
teeth blacked out, and was the hit of the evening—despite
the fact that Mr. Berle is more than three thousand miles
away. Walter and I are not in accord politically. He favors
the administration that is in office now, while I favor the one
that is momentarily out. He favors the opinion of the Secretary of State, who has made statements to the effect that in
the Middle East, Egypt is our friend. The secretary definitely
emphasized this when he visited the premier of Egypt (now
in the can) and brought him a silver revolver as a token of
the esteem of the American people. (I don't recall the American people chipping in to buy this pistol!) I, of course, don't
in any way go along with the secretary's policy in the Middle
East, and I have been given to understand that Walter does.
I cannot believe that these pagan countries, that have held
back civilization for thousands of years, that have spent an

eternity in the market places smoking strange weeds and eating goat-doodle, are the friends of modern democracy. There are some things that Winchell and myself do agree upon—that Zanuck is quite a guy and that certain ladies are easy on the eye. But even if we didn't agree on anything, knowing a man forty-five years forges a bond of such great strength that a political or theatrical opinion cannot break it in two. No, gentlemen, everything old becomes a thing religious, and, by a strange irony, ivy often climbs on the wall of an old deserted brothel long before it does on a young church. So be it. I now present to you the most listened-to newspaperman of our time, Walter Winchell . . ."

Of the youngsters on TV, there are two fellows I like very much—one completely a product of the channels, the other from the borsch circuit and the bistros. Robert Q. Lewis never tries too hard, never makes you nervous, and because the studio audiences are nearly always receptive, he has never learned to do what we call "punch," which you have to do so often with a paying audience that is a little cold. The other young fellow is Red Buttons, who I think has been pushed too quickly and has had too much pressure put on him, so that his demeanor often suggests that he has been a star as long as Eddie Cantor instead of an up-and-coming, very talented kid. He has also suffered greatly from whoever has handled his studio audiences. When he comes on and says hello, I've heard and watched them scream, applaud, and whistle for at least two minutes; and his every line—whether it be a straight one or the tiniest little gag —makes them scream with laughter, as if they were watching a happy and sane Charlie Chaplin in *The Gold Rush*. I hope Buttons finds the right kind of thinking and management. He is a sweet and talented boy. As for the others, Jackie Gleason was a fine actor a long time ago and at this writing

I have just heard and watched George Gobel. He hasn't been on much longer than a kiss on the silent screen but shows a very literate sense of comedy. I hope the powers that rule do not throttle it.

And to all the rest of the lads—Happy Ratings to you!

Honey, through the good graces or the idio-syncrasies of the American public, I've been able to take you all through Europe and the Middle East twice in the dozen years of your life—at ten and at twelve—and while we didn't scream and wave the flag when we saw the Statue of Liberty, or kiss the ground at Idlewild when we returned home, we were certainly glad to get back.

Yes, this is the land to live in, and that's why I get so mad at the people who try to harm it. And why I've written the following.

7. Affectionately, U.S.A.

For a long time I had been vitally disturbed, along with many other at least halfway-thinking people, by a series of books written about principal cities of the U.S.A., —confidential metropolis this and confidential city that— written without any regard for the truth or without even the knowledge of the geography of these places.

In conversations with groups of people and in clubs I often brought this up, and then was calmed down by most of them with their telling me, "Nobody but an awfully stupid person would pay any attention to these pieces . . ."

So I just let my fire go out.

But on my last two trips abroad, particularly the one I made just some months ago, I have found that these pamphlets of lies about the United States in general have caused much more ill feeling and might be responsible for more international incidents showing disrespect for us than any of the remarks made by all the Americans who disagreed with critics, newspapermen, and statesmen in Europe since the day of Benjamin Franklin.

These books are as close to treason as anything I've ever read, for traveling through Europe ever so often the American is told, or can gather by knowing a little of a foreign language, that Americans should be well satisfied with the services they receive in Europe, even if their bills and checks are not always accurately counted. Because in our own country there are nothing but hoodlums, crooks, and white-slavers all over the place; that the police and most of the high officials in every city are corrupt and are former lieutenants in Al Capone's gang who nightly divide the spoils through a long pipe system which goes to Frank Costello's den in New York; and he, in turn, divides them up with Dutch Schultz and Lucky Luciano (this, despite the fact that Schultz is dead and Lucky lives very quietly in Italy selling neckties).

The readers of these books throughout Europe—and particularly the youth of the countries—are told about Chicago as if the times of thirty years ago are happening right now —and even those times have been exaggerated. They are told that a stone's throw from the Sherman Hotel is the Edgewater Beach, where there is a series of streets with nothing but brothels and gambling houses. That is about as true as the distance of a stone's throw between the two hotels, which actually takes more than a half-hour in a fast taxicab.

Readers of this claptrap are told about bookmakers being all over the place and make bookmaking seem a terrible crime, which amazes the average Englishman or Frenchman who can call up his bookmaker or meet him on the street, make a bet, and it is perfectly legitimate. Therefore, the European believes that our American bookmaker, since he is such a criminal, must either pay off in counterfeit money or shoot the winning horses as they come down the stretch. And that practically everything in America is a racket, and a rotten one.

I truly believe that any mother and father in Europe, who have read four or five of these books about America being nothing but a series of corrupt cities from the capitol down, will shudder at the thought of letting their ambitious young come to this great country, whereas in the past, they prayed for such a journey for themselves and their kids.

I even believe my good friend Senator Kefauver here at home was taken in by this trash on paper, and although in his tour throughout the country he did some good, it was not enough to make up for the bad name we received all over the world.

And I also believe that certain newspapers of our own are responsible for the birth of more young gangsters than Prohibition or poverty ever achieved, by their building up the high life and big profits of crime through continued headlines about gangsters making millions, that every tough kid with a gat can make enough money to buy a yacht, a string of race horses, and the control of a railroad in no time at all.

In the senator's appearance in Los Angeles and in other cities where he spoke on TV and held court on TV, fellows who bet a two-dollar bill in a baseball park were put on trial under the lights (without make-up, of course), photographed continuously and made to seem like people who would have kidnaped the Lindbergh child and shot President McKinley every morning before breakfast, without a qualm.

But the books have done the most damage, for I don't believe my friend, the senator from Tennessee, really believes that his country has so many villains in it, and in his heart he is much too wise and tolerant to actually believe that if you have one foot inside any race track, it is legal to bet a million dollars, but should your foot slip outside and you bet one dollar, you are a terrible criminal, and that that dollar is being cut up between the police and the high officials of the cities.

Being as keyed up on this as I have always been, on my return from Europe I first thought of writing an article or trying to make myself heard by a letter to the New York *Times* and other important newspapers. Then I was told, "You shouldn't do this because the man who dreamed up these books was a friend of yours, and is no longer on the scene to defend his works . . ." That doesn't make any sense. All of my friends are not infallible, and some that have passed on were not quite a combination of Nathan Straus, Stonewall Jackson, Young Wild West, and Sister Kenny . . . and there is no reason for anyone to believe that the passing of a man pardons all things.

I remember an incident apropos . . .

Many years ago, when James "Jimmy" Walker was the mayor of New York, I was "without portfolio" his representative on practically all speaking occasions. If he could attend, I would carry the ball till he got there, and then present him; if he couldn't attend, I spoke in his place.

On this one occasion he called me to meet him early the following morning to go to Albany, and speak with him at a political luncheon in the Ten Eyck Hotel. The world was not flying then, so we took the train. We arrived at the hotel just a few minutes before the luncheon was to begin. His Honor the Mayor of New York *Cohanesquely* strutted through the lobby. I was close at his heels, but not quick enough to duck a man who was as stewed at twelve o'clock noon as the ordinary fellow would be in a month of continuous schnopsing . . . He grabbed me and said, "Georgie, you going to talk here today?" I said, "Yes, I am—I am going to introduce the speakers and then His Honor the Mayor." He said, "Well, listen, kid—be sure you say something nice about Mike Malloy. He kicked the bucket a couple of days ago. None of these guys appreciate what a great fellow he was—and I am depending on you to talk about him." I said, "Okay, kid, I'll do the best I can . . ."

The luncheon was soon over as far as the food was concerned, the coffee was poured, and the speaking began. I introduced several state senators and leaders of the party, and every time I sat down, I'd get a note from my *shikker* friend: "When are you going to talk about Mike Malloy?"

Toward the end of the luncheon he crawled over to the dais and under the table pulled at my trouser legs and said, "What about Mike?" And crawled out again.

The next speaker was a celebrated judge from New York, whose speech was all about Jimmy Walker, and about the mayor's coming birthday. This speech was much too long, so much so that when he was finished, I thanked him and said, "I only hope Mayor Walker lives as long as your speech." However, during his long oratorical tour I inquired from a man sitting near me about Mike Malloy, and was told that he was a pretty tough guy and had certainly been of no help to the party.

So, before I closed the meeting, I addressed the gathering as follows: ". . . and before we adjourn, gentlemen, I must tell you that since my arrival here, I have been asked by one of those present several times to say a word about a Mr. Mike Malloy. I not only have been asked to say something, I have almost had my pants pulled off under the table. I find that Mr. Malloy left the scene just a few days ago and went on to his Maker—quite unexpectedly—but I must say in all honesty that his hasty exit from the play of life doesn't excuse his bad performance . . . Good afternoon, gentlemen, and may we meet again under such happy Democratic circumstances."

I hadn't even finished when my inebriated pal came to me, threw his arms around me, and tears streaming down his cheek, said, "I knew I could depend upon you—I'll never forget you for speaking so nice about Mike Malloy."

Therefore my old friend and his collaborators, whether here or beyond, are not to be forgiven for these supposed inside facts on the very great American cities being one large plaza of iniquity. They have done their country a great disservice, and if their idea was: "We wanted to make money, and the end has justified the means . . ." I am not sure that it was so. Very often those who live by the code of "the end justifying the means" find themselves not the beneficiary of the end, but the victim of the means.

Jeri, the other day, while you were imitating Doris Day's record of "My Secret Love," I was thinking of the imitations that I used to do on the stage when I was your age. My first ones were of Eddie Foy, the comedian, and of David Warfield, the great tragicomedian.

Most of the mimics today are caricaturing and not imitating the new people like Johnnie Ray and Jerry Lewis, and a great many are still doing us older folk—Cantor, Richman, and me. But the most imitated men in the history of the American amusement world have been George M. Cohan and Al Jolson, despite the fact that they are no longer on this stage. I was with them both almost to the end. Let me tell you a bit about George and more about Al.

8. King George and King Jolie

IN MY MORE THAN FOUR DECADES of living and working in show business, the two greatest natural talents I've ever met were George M. Cohan and Al Jolson.

Mr. Cohan was known for his great creative work as actor, author, composer, and his benevolence toward fellow actors; yet no one really knew him personally—or got really deep inside him—except on rare occasions a couple of us, in the small hours of the morning in the Oak Room of the Plaza Hotel in New York—where incidentally, after George's and Sam Harris' passing, I placed a plaque which was suggested to me by the head waiter who night after night, for years and years, had served George, Sam, and me. My name dedicated the plaque. One night, however, through some pre-meditated vandalism, we found the plaque had been taken off, and a short time later a plaque was put up by the Lambs' Club about their great fellow member George M. Cohan (no mention of Sam Harris) and of course, all Broadway, with the exception of the younger group of the Lambs, sardonically smiled. For if ever a man disliked an organization and a group of men, Cohan did the Lambs . . . and it was only in the last few years of his life, with the Old Friars' monastery gone, that he walked into the Lambs, and I believe he was a member of it at the time of his passing.

When George was a young man and a vaudevillian, he tried to join the club, but was blackballed. Later on, when he became a great success, he was invited to join. He did and was so unhappy about it that this prompted him to build the Friars into the greatest theatrical organization the world would ever know. At all of the Friars shindigs there was not one that did not have a jibe or a sarcastic dart at the Lambs and its high-falutin membership.

And everyone in the know knew how George felt about the Lambs up until the time when he was getting too mellow to remember any unkindnesses of the past.

I, too, was once blackballed by the Lambs and then invited to join. I was a Lamb for a few days, then after the Oak Room incident I resigned, and I believe I owe a few days' dues, which I will pay some time when I get my money back that I invested with Chico Marx in his uranium mines in Newark, New Jersey.

Believe me, this is not any condemnation of the present roster of the Lambs' Club. I wouldn't dare say anything unkind about a building that serves as a hangout for actors, old and young. There are so few places for us to play and to hang out where we can rest our elbows, drink our ale, and then grit our teeth and go out and shoulder the television skies.

Now let me tell you about King Jolie . . .

Later in this book there is a eulogy that I spoke at his bier. If one has the time or the interest to re-read it and analyze it, one will surely find that while, from a holy place, I honestly lamented the passing of this great, great, dynamic personality and talent and his impact on the theater world, I never ventured much about the man himself. For Jolie too, like most men of extraordinary ability, was a man with many idiosyncrasies, and nobody got under his skin.

I met him the first time when I was eleven years old, in San Francisco. I was playing in a kid act called "Gus Edwards' Kid Cabaret" with Eddie Cantor. Cantor was doing an imitation of Jolson, who that year—it was 1913—was already a star of the Winter Garden.

Several years intervened, and it was not until 1919 that we met again. He was touring the country in a play called *Big Boy*, and I had a vaudeville act, "Georgie Jessel's Troubles." If business was good—and it always was with Al, with the possible exception of an off night in Syracuse or a snowstorm in Des Moines—and if the stock market was good and if Al was beating all of his gang in the card game, Hearts, and the horses, Al was in good humor. He loved to talk a lot about old times and old-timers, and he particularly got a great kick when I would give imitations of comedians who sang like Harry Cooper—a famous actor—who appeared on the stage as an old Jewish man, with a long beard and a derby on his head, and then sang in a rich, high tenor voice that was always a surprise to the audience. The first words of one of his old songs goes like this:

"In the green fields of Virginia
in the vale of Shenandoah . . ."

Al would get such a kick out of this mimicry that I might be playing in Spokane, Washington, and the phone would ring from Norfolk, Virginia, and Louis Epstein—Jolson's manager and devoted servant for many years—would get on and say in a very perfunctory manner, "Al wants to hear a few bars of Harry Cooper . . ." I would sing a few bars, and Eppy would say, "Al says thanks, and he will see you in New York." This happened once or twice a week for a whole season.

You can't say that Jolson was an egocentric. Most men love themselves—and I believe it was La Rochefoucauld or Ed Sullivan who said: "A man must love himself, for this is the only lifelong romance . . ." Egocentric is too small a word for Jolson. Nature had somehow contrived him to be particularly immune to anyone else's pains and problems, so that he was only affected by what was happening to him at that particular moment. I can't believe he wanted to be like that, but nevertheless he was. As in the truthful portrayal of his life story on the screen, he was only content while singing and acknowledging applause; the rest of the time he was champing at the bit while getting ready to go on—and if he was not on, he was disconsolate.

The word "failure" in connection with anything he had to do with was something he never uttered. At a horse race, in the stock market, at the ball game, you would always hear Jolson had a winner—even if you knew he hadn't. I remember once we were going to the races at Belmont Park on Long Island. We came late, just as the first race was over, and sat down to have a sandwich. They were just putting up the numbers on the board: who was first, second, and third. A man passing through the restaurant said, "Hello, boys. Did you have the winner, Al?" and Al characteristically said, "I didn't have his sister . . . I didn't bet much here, but I bet a big chunk with a Sleepy Joe in Cincinnati." "Well, you got a good price," said the man, "she was eight to one." And Al whispered to me, "Find out who won. I don't know what goat he is talking about."

At the race track, I am sure you know, people walk around. You see one race from somebody's box, another race from the lawn, and I didn't get back to Al until the last race, and we drove home together. I said, "Al, how did you do?" And he answered, "Never had a loser. You know I started off good with that first race—that eight-to-one shot."

Right after the stock-market crash I met him. Cantor and I and almost everyone else had gone broke, and Al said, "I was lucky . . . I sold nearly everything the day before the crash."

On the romantic side this was something!

After one of his marriages, which was a highly romantic episode, he and some of his cronies came to my dressing room at the theater, where I was playing in *The War Song*. I asked him about his lady fair, how she was feeling, and so on, and he said, "I don't know how she is . . ." So, I said: "How can you say that—you've just come back from your honeymoon in Europe. Aren't you in love?" And he said, "What love? Who wants to go to Europe alone?" He wouldn't even give in that he could love somebody.

During the intervals when he was a bachelor, we used to drive to Atlantic City for the week ends. One night we were the judges at a Charleston Contest, and awarded prizes to two young ladies who were the winners—Miss Ruby Stevens and Miss Mae Clarke. Al was quite taken by Miss Stevens. She was young, she could dance, she was pretty, and notwithstanding that she later changed her name to Barbara Stanwyck, she had more authority and carriage than the average Charleston dancer by far.

We rode in wheel chairs along the Boardwalk at night. I, as per custom, started reciting the Indian Love Lyrics to Miss Clarke, but Al's way of wooing Miss Stevens was particularly his own and went something like this: "Honey, it's a funny thing, your name being Stevens. That's the name of the president of one of my banks that I got six million dollars in . . ." And perhaps later Miss Stevens might say, "I just got a letter from my aunt in Washington. Do you mind if I read it?" And Jolson would say, "Go ahead—I just got ten thousand shares of American Tel and Tel."

Miss Stevens, while quite flattered by Jolson's interest in her, did not go completely overboard, despite the fact that he made several week-end trips to Atlantic City to see her. Al had a suite at the Ritz-Carlton Hotel in New York City, and I had an adjoining room, and one morning, by mistake, I opened a telegram that had been shoved under my door and it read as follows: *Dear Al—thanks for the flowers. If you are coming this week end to see me, please don't, as I have to keep other engagements. Fondly—Ruby.* I naturally sealed up the telegram and slipped it under Al's door, and while we were having breakfast, I said, "How about Atlantic City?" He said, "No, it wouldn't be fair to that little girl. No use keeping her stuck on me, when I am only kidding her. I just got a telegram this morning saying, *Al, if you don't come up and see me, I'll just die* . . . I just wired her back: *Sorry, honey, I can't make it.*"

He could be terriby kind but terribly cruel to those who served him. You were his pal one moment and the next a complete stranger working for him. The last few years most people would say, "Isn't Al getting mellow?" But he was not getting mellow, he was just getting older.

At a dinner given to me after I had functioned in more than a dozen in honor of him, Al came on, made a speech, and then sang several songs to the delight of the audience. And then, just to make it tougher for me, who had to make the last speech, he said, "Folks, I'll stay on all night if you want me." And I jumped up and said, "No, you won't . . . this is my dinner and you sit down."

Fellows who are not in the know say he loved me. He didn't. He respected my ability to talk and recognized the fact that having read a great deal, nine chances out of ten I would know what I was talking about.

No one will ever be able to understand that in his will he left great sums of money to colleges and organizations with which he had had no association or admiration for. This is something to conjure with. But more so!—the fact that the two men in whose arms he practically breathed his last breath on earth—one who had been with him over thirty-five years, the other not so long a time, but who had toured the encampments all over the world with him and acted as his buddy and accompanist, and even his music director—to these men who nightly played cards with him, rubbed his back for him, dined with him, soothed all of the wounds that sometimes hurt his vanity, took his gals home for him, visited his own relatives for him, served him like loving brothers as well as if he had been a Roman emperor and they his slaves —to these two men he left nothing. Not even a token of a tiny ring or a cuff link or a pin or a portrait. Even his music arranger and warm confidant for twenty years who was also at his death bed; he neither received a farthing or a remembrance. He left all his jewels, from beautiful black pearls down to a most masculine set of baseball cuff links,

to people who were practically strangers—and more important, who needed none of these gifts. Yet, despite the fact
that the three old buddies of his were anything but rich, it
was being completely forgotten that broke their hearts—not
the monetary consideration.

What cruel twist there was in his last gesture of showing
that no pal or relative meant anything to him, no one will
ever know. Yet, I miss him . . . and find that despite everything, including the many cruel things that he did to me
and he said to me, I miss him. Definitely he must have stated
long before he passed on that he didn't want me to eulogize
him because it took the late Johnny Hyde—who represented
Al in several ventures—Ben Holzman, and the entire gang
of the William Morris office, to convince his sweet widow
that the theatrical profession had chosen me to speak. He
didn't even want me at the finish. Just as, at the height of
his success, when nothing could possibly affect him, he hated
to hear about anyone else making a hit, from an act with
trained dogs to a fat soprano. Yet I miss him. For he was
so good to look at . . . and he seemed so strong and like
such an impregnable thing—and I miss him! And I forgive
him for many things.

Like someone said of Tchaikowsky, "He is a snob," and
another replied, "Yes, but God, what beautiful music he
writes . . ." So of Jolson. He was cruel most times . . . but
God, what a great artist he was!

*Young lady, I've just reserved a seat on the
plane to go to San Francisco to meet you, your mother,
and your fine stepdad, so that we may celebrate your
birthday. I planned a dinner with cake and candles at
the Fairmount Hotel, and it is possible that the pro-
prietor of the hotel, dear Ben Swigg, may give us the
cake compliments de la maison. And my sweet old rich
friend Louis R. Lurie may at least help you blow out
the candles and eat a large portion of the cake.*

*I guess I've made at least one hundred airplane trips
from Los Angeles to San Francisco and back. But on
one occasion I had an experience, and as the saying
goes, "here's one for the book—"*

9. The Belly Landing

I DOUBT WHETHER there is anyone in our time
who has flown as many air miles as I have in the last few
years. I would say that I've averaged six to seven thousand
miles a week, what with my commuting from Los Angeles
to New York, and my quick and many trips over most of
the world.

I've only had two accidents that might have had a fatal
ending, and both of these lean toward the comic rather than
toward the tragic side—at least as far as I am concerned.
There is an interesting thing about actors and actresses,
which is that they have less fear in most cases because they
don't quite realize the reality of things. I once told General
Marshall that I thought that actors who were in the service
should be chosen for dangerous expeditions, because their
first thought will be: "Think of the notices I'll get." I can

just see an actor now, ordered to go over the trenches to deliver a message through enemy fire, and as he climbs up the parapet, you can bet ten to one he will pause first as if waiting for a spotlight or the camera to move up.

I say this because that is how I felt when, on one occasion, high above the ground, I was told to get ready to bail out, and on another when I was told that we would make a crash landing, which means without any wheels—the ship just coming in on its belly, and the rest is a guess as to who will meet you when you land: a blonde or the undertaker.

For instance, after I had spoken at the Inaugural Dinner given in honor of Mr. Truman and Mr. Barkley in Washington in 1949, I was a pretty tired fellow. I had been in Washington for a few days before the shindig, and to a lot of parties after. Therefore, still in my striped pants, frock coat, and high hat, I flew to New York in time to get the sleeper plane to Los Angeles. When I arrived at the airport at La Guardia Field, there was a large package waiting for me from Siegel's Delicatessen Restaurant, New York. The box contained mostly salami, green tomatoes, and sliced corned beef, all of which contained enough garlic to almost cover Texas. It was too late to check this package, and I was so knocked out that I carried it into my berth, took a tiny sleeping pill, a drink, and was asleep within three minutes. It seemed but a moment later that I felt the stewardess pulling at my arm, but it actually was hours, about three-thirty in the morning. She said, "We think the ship is on fire—get ready to deplane." Still filled with Washington oratory and the schnapps and the sleeping pill, I remember mumbling, ". . . and you have awakened me to say you *think* the ship is on fire? I am going back to sleep, and when you *know* it is on fire, call me again."

Anyway, we came down on an emergency landing field, and wherever or whatever the fire was, it was put out. We immediately changed planes. I had to put on the striped pants, frock coat, and high hat, take the brief case and the box of delicatessen, and get into another berth. But the refrigeration, or air-conditioning, didn't come through for some time, so that the box, with the salami and green tomatoes and other stuffs, began to manifest its aroma. Just as I went to sleep, the stewardess came through and said, "Mr. Jessel, this odor is annoying people. What do you have in that box?" I told her that I was dreadfully sorry, but that my uncle, a midget, had passed away in the East, and I was bringing him back to California.

But as I looked around my personal things after I got home, I noticed that my *mezuzah* was missing. (A *mezuzah* is a religious token—you may have seen it on the doors of many Jewish homes.) Actually, it means *doorpost*. Most of them are about an inch long and have a portion of the Scriptures and often the Commandments inside, with a little opening that shows one holy Hebrew letter. This particular one had been given to me by a group of children in Allentown, Pennsylvania, and I treasured it.

A day or two later the airline wrote to me:

Dear Mr. Jessel. In cleaning up the ship in which you started your journey, we found your little gold whistle, which we are returning in a box to you. You should probably receive it by next mail. Very cordially yours.

I wondered how anybody could have described a holy *mezuzah* as a whistle. I discovered later that a couple of young fellows who cleaned out the plane found it. One said to the other, "What is that thing with a little hole in it?" The other said, "It is a whistle and no wonder it won't blow. There's a piece of paper stuck inside it." Whereupon they took the parchment out, tried the whistle, gave it up, and a few days later I had an empty *mezuzah*.

This incident I remember so much more often than the

fact of the fire in the plane, which might have forced us to ditch and might have proved the end.

The belly landing was much more dangerous. This happened about a year later, and what transpired on the plane and in the minds and the actions of the people kept reminding me of a play called *The Deluge* and the book *The Bridge of San Luis Rey,* wherein a group of people have the same problem confronting them. Strangely, the book and the picture, *The High and the Mighty,* is as close to the tale that I tell now as if its author had been on the plane with me. The only difference is that my journey was to be about two hours long, from San Francisco to Los Angeles—not from Honolulu—two hours, just about the time it takes to see the picture *The High and the Mighty* or read the book.

I was returning with the late Charles Skouras, president of Fox West-coast Theatres, and some of his managers. I had spoken at their convention in San Francisco. We were all very gay. With our group of about twelve, the plane was fully seated: fifty-two passengers in all. We had a few little nips during the trip and lots of laughs, and suddenly, before we knew it, the sign came on: "Fasten your seat belts," which means that the plane is descending for a landing. We started to descend and then, a moment later, the plane swooped up. Then the sign went off, and we started circling the airfield—which, as a rule, means that there is a great deal of traffic and planes have to wait and circle around for a bit.

However, after a half-hour of circling around, there was no question that something was wrong. I got up out of my seat and walked up to the front of the plane to ask the captain what was going on, and during this walk I had time to say a word or two to some of the passengers, some of whom had recognized me.

There was a sailor and his girl, who were going away to

make a quick marriage. There were a couple of gamblers en route to Las Vegas. There was a man and his wife who had been throwing mean looks at each other in the airport and were arguing as they had boarded the plane. My seat partner was Mr. Skouras, a fine and happy-go-lucky man but a strict disciplinarian about his theaters, and he had made up his mind that some of the gentlemen who were making the trip with us would soon be out of his company.

The information I received from the captain was that he would make an announcement in a few moments, and there was nothing to worry about. However, another half-hour went by and we were still circling, and by this time there was a little nervousness all around, everybody anxiously peering out of the plane windows. And then the captain came out and made this announcement: "There seems to be something wrong with our landing gear, which won't come down. However, while we are circling, with the help of one or two of you, we may be able to get it to work by hand." Whereupon they started to rip open the floor of the plane in order to get to the landing gear. But it would not work.

By this time we had been circling for three hours, and in circling around we had made many dips and turns and most of the passengers were becoming ill, some so sick that the stewardess had to use every first-aid available for air sickness, including the giving out of oxygen masks. We were then told that we might have to go back to San Francisco, but that if the weather turned bad there, we might try for Albuquerque—but they were not sure, as they didn't know whether they had enough gas for that trip.

By now we were four hours over our scheduled arrival time, and all the occupants of the plane had but one line of thought: Will we fall, will we crash, and will we die? And what about the people who were waiting for us at the airport, and those who expected us home, and those who by this time might have heard it over the radio as it was being broadcast that we were in trouble in the air?

There was no news for another half-hour. And then came a speech from the captain, in the same warm, make-you-feel-confident manner of John Wayne and Bobby Stack (in the movie) telling us that what they might do would be to fly over the ocean, ditch all the gas, and make a crash landing. The captain said that he and his copilot had gone through this a couple of times, and they were sure it would work out all right. He would let us know a little later if and when we were going to do so.

And now the passengers reacted as all humans do under the stress of circumstances—lamenting for mistakes of the past, promises to do better in future, blaming themselves and then everybody else for this predicament.

The sailor and his bride-to-be, who had been smooching almost all the way, were now holding each other at a distance, the girl crying, "I am being punished because I didn't tell my father and mother . . . it's all your fault. I should never have let you talk me into this . . ."; the boy saying, "It is not my fault—it was your idea as well as mine." The two gamblers reacted entirely unexpectedly. One took out a rosary and started to pray; the other one I heard say, "Get me in on it, because I don't know how . . ." The married couple were in a clinch, she crying on his shoulder and he saying, "Don't worry, honey—whatever happens, we are together." Charlie Skouras told his men that not only would none of them be fired, but when we arrived safely, he had a pleasant surprise for them when they came to their offices on Monday. And in my ear he whispered, "I'll raise their salaries . . ."

Then came the bombshell! All of us were to go to the back of the plane, the fifty-two of us, and huddle as close as sardines, the stewardess would tie a rope around us, and we were going to crash-land.

For the next few minutes all of us held on to each other. Believe it or not, the reality of all this didn't quite hit me until we were tied up. Before that I had been passing the time reviewing some love scenes I had played off the stage —and when I got back to one leading lady for the second time, my thoughts changed to the grim reality of the moment. But I believed fully that nothing was going to happen to us.

As we came down, the landing gear, through some happy trick of circumstance, had partly emerged, and we landed, shook and spun a tiny bit, and the engines were stopped.

There was not a word spoken till we started leaving the plane, and as we did, we saw surrounding us fire engines, ambulances, and men dressed in asbestos clothes because, as a rule, a plane immediately catches fire after a crash.

There were, of course, newspapermen, and there were pictures taken of me kissing the pilot, and of Skouras with his arms around his men. And then we slowly walked toward the airport to wait for our baggage. The sailor and the girl started smooching again, the man and his wife were having some little argument about who had the baggage checks, the gamblers had rushed to a newsstand to get the results of the last race at Bay Meadows, Skouras was telling his men to be sure and get in early Monday morning, he had something to say to them, and there was going to be no fooling around about it, as the conditions at certain theaters were deplorable.

And I walked up into the Sky Room saloon and had two boilermakers (ingredients: two whiskies and two bottles of beer).

During the past few weeks we have traveled many leagues—from Cannes to Canaan; we've dunked in Coney Island and also in the Aegean Sea.

You, Jeri, would sometimes lay down Gone with the Wind and jot something down on your diary. This you haven't shown me, and I wonder if it would make any sense even to you, because you were so absorbed in the novel. I know you liked Paris and had much more interest in Fontainebleau and the Louvre than you did the last time. And in Rome, also, the historic things and the open-air opera ran a closer second to Margaret Mitchell than it did in the other countries. When we walked up to the Parthenon in Athens and your daddy was breathing rather heavily, I think you said something like this: "Rhett Butler could have climbed these steps in a minute!"

And one midnight in Jerusalem when the howling of the hungry dogs from over the border kept us awake, I asked you if you were frightened, and you said, "Why, no. Would Scarlett O'Hara be frightened?"

Anyway, this is the mental diary that I made during our trip, and maybe someday you will let me compare it with yours. And I'd like to bet yours would go something like this: "Dear Mummy: We've just arrived at Milano, where the wonderful Opera House, La Scala, is, and where Caruso and all the great stars used to sing——" And probably your next paragraph would be: "The Civil War is over and the O'Hara family is having an awful time . . ."

Anyway, here's what your daddy thinks about our last trip abroad.

10. From Cannes to Canaan

L ET'S GO TO FRANCE:

Paris, despite the fact that it has been practically occupied by enemies three times in eighty years, has not changed too much. The Champs-Elysées is still the most colorful thoroughfare in the world; Mona Lisa's eyes still follow you all over the Louvre; the Arc de Triomphe still stands as proud as if anxious to welcome Napoleon; the theater is practically the same, although the girls in the Folies Bergère are not nearly as pretty as they were in former years—with the exception of Yvonne Menard. The French movies have improved tremendously, Sacha Guitry, at seventy, having the time of his life as actor, author, and director; and the prices in restaurants are even higher than an elephant's eye.

As for politics, there seems to be a very strong man at the head of the government, Pierre Mendès-France. His administration looks to be a very stable one, in great contrast to the many political regimes before him, which seemed to have been run by the Marx Brothers assisted by Jerry Lewis.

As for the threat of communism, I believe this to be a very tiny threat, if any. The Frenchman who owns his little farm and garden holds it too close to his heart, and his pocket, to have it be the property of the state, with him being merely a janitor. There are only, I believe, about twenty per cent of the people who are white-collar folk and who are and have been terribly underpaid through the years and therefore are fertile soil for any kind of a change for the better—but certainly not for communism as it is in Russia.

The French feeling about America and Americans is actually based on what they read and hear. The McCarthy-Army bit lost us a great deal of prestige—the man on the street was sure there were too many Commies in our Military, and that McCarthy had much more authority than a senator should have, and was a dictator in the making. They think President Eisenhower is a fine man, completely under the will of his political party, and that he seems more of a chairman of the board of a large corporation than the presidents before him—particularly the two before him.

The South of France, the Riviera, is much the same as in former years: a little less stylish perhaps, but it has not lost its swank as much as our Palm Beach.

As to war in the offing, this is the last thing in the Frenchman's mind. Of course he does not want it, and upon hearing some of us Yankee-doodling in the better bistros about what we ought to do to our enemy right away, the Frenchman says, "You people in America have not been hurt enough to understand what war means. If you had been compelled to shrink in your bellies and watch the Nazis goose-stepping up Broadway, as we had to watch them down the Champs-Elysées, you might act a litte more slowly."

American tourists must beware of only one thing on their first trip to Paris, and that is the buying of francs from someone on the street, instead of getting them in the legitimate manner from the bank or the hotel or the Express Companies. For some of the five-thousand-franc notes pur-

chased from the guys on the corner soon turn out to be nice
old leaves of lettuce.

And now, for ITALY:

First and always, Rome. Here, also, are the people not
excited about anything much, except their own economy.
As for the arts, the opera is technically better than it ever
was. The movies are much more active, and Donney's street
café next to the Hotel Excelsior reminds the showman of
the old days in the Astor Hotel in New York where many
fortunes were made at the luncheon tables—but only on the
tablecloth.

The political scene seems to be the same as in former
years, the Red problem is about the same as it is in France
—only perhaps a little louder because of the natural *fortis-
simo* of Italian voices. The prices for Americans are just
about as high as in France, except that the porters and
waiters seem to smile a little more gratefully.

Italy is in no way married to the past. The only things
old are the Colosseum, and the few remaining pillars in
the old Forum. The thinking of the average Italian goes
back only about as far as the early times of Sophie Tucker
and not Tiberius. I think this is exemplified in the following
experience:

I came down one morning and said to the beautifully
uniformed major-domo in front of the hotel, "Why is it I
hear nothing or see nothing relative to Caesar—the great
one, Julius. Where is he buried?"

He was a little bit preoccupied with other duties, but
when he heard something of what I had said, he replied,
"Buried? You mean he is dead?"

"I imagine so," I said.

"Just a minute," he said. He attended to some other duty
and then continued. "I am going to have you talk to that

taximan, Joe. He has been around here about 30 years—he knows everybody. Maybe he can tell you."

He called Joe over in Italian and said something to the effect that I wanted to know about a man called Caesar, and where he was buried . . .

Joe, the taximan, said, "I know him—he is notta dead . . . He went to Palermo to see his brother. He issa-sick . . ."

So I said, "You mean his brother Morris Caesar?" and Joe said, "Yes, I think so."

That night I went to see my friend Maurice Chevalier at the Casino della Rosa. He was anxiously awaiting news about his return to America and wondering if he were still remembered there. And of course I told him, "You certainly are, Maurice—but look what has happened here. I can't find anybody who knows a thing about Julius Caesar: where he is buried, where he was murdered . . . I don't see a statue or a bust anywhere."

Maurice said, "The assistant manager of this place is coming here. I am sure he will know something about it."

Almost on cue he came, and I hit him immediately with: "Does anybody know anything about Caesar? Where is he buried—what——" When I got that far, he said, "I think I know the man you mean, and he is all right. He lives at the Hotel Eden—but he goes to sleep very early. You want to call him, call him in the morning."

There was no need to go further into the conversation. I called up the Associated Press in Rome the following morning, and nobody knew much about it there either, except that some people say the Great Caesar was killed in the Forum, others in a secret meeting room used by Roman Senators. Some of the opinion was that he had been cremated and his ashes strewn somewhere outside of Rome. But I could find nothing authentic. I finished my interview with the Associated Press by saying, "If people so quickly forget, even Willie Mays will be forgotten in America when four or five thousand years have gone by . . ."

And now to GREECE:

Where almost everything that we know began: Christianity, philosophy, culture, and all of the arts combined. Homer, Plato, Socrates, Euripides, and in our time, Charles, George, and Spyros Skouras.

The city of Athens is the happiest metropolis that I visited in the Old World. When one awakens in the morning, he is not sure whether or not he is still in a dream, for looking out of the window of the most modern hotel, he can almost reach his hand out and touch the Acropolis and the Parthenon—and if your trousers on the chair suddenly turned into a toga, you wouldn't be a bit surprised.

Summer nights on Athens' seashore beggar description. There are literally hundreds of little restaurants and cafés, each with a singer or a band of musicians, or both, one after the other as far as the eye can see—as many as the hotels in Miami Beach.

The Greek admiration for America and its people is a very full one.

And now, to the Holy Land—ISRAEL:

First, regardless of what your religious beliefs may be, you must prepare yourself to be completely disillusioned. If you think that in the streets of Jerusalem you will see the giants of the Scriptures and men looking like Michaelangelo's Moses, then you have another Scripture coming. And if you think that you are going to see people whose eyes are in the clouds and who are looking forward to sundown so that they can caress their praying shawls, you've got another prayer coming. The people of Israel are a seething group of hard-working, ambitious-to-survive humans.

Most of them have gone through hell and have no wish to get anywhere near there again. Because of that they will fight to their last breath. Here too, in a country not any bigger than Connecticut, with musket fire heard dimly from nearby borders, there does not seem to be any thought of war in the offing—at least as far as the people are concerned. The confidence of the young boys and girls in the Army is akin to the great sense of humor of the people. I said to a boy no more than twenty, a soldier, "Do you think you will have war, and if so, how will you fare?" His answer was, "If we are outnumbered five to one, we will win, but if it is more than that, we will have to use weapons."

There is but one train in Israel, a three-coacher, daily, which happily whistles itself from Jerusalem to Haifa. Because its tracks are so close to unfriendly borders, there is a sign in one of the coaches that reads: "Passengers are cautioned not to stick their heads out of the state." I came close to some Arab shooting early one morning, and it is very annoying, even though the marksmanship of the enemy is not very accurate. They aim at a group of Jews and hit one goat a mile away.

Yes, the people who come to Israel looking for much piety and prayer will see and hear nothing of the sort. There is one small overreligious sect who believes in doing nothing but reading the holy books and who are fanatic about the Sabbath. Every once in a while one of them lies down in the middle of the street as if to give a general warning that there should be no motor cars or wagons driven on the Sabbath, but they are getting fewer and fewer, and the Yemeni children, whose sideburns are so long that they have to be braided under their chins, will soon be shaving them off and in a short while will be playing football and baseball.

Yes, freedom makes a great change in a people, particularly these folk from all over Europe and Asia, who suddenly have come upon our modern era in all its fullness—and yet have gone into it with everything. In a book called *Solal,* written in French by Albert Cohen, many years ago, he says, "Alas, poor Israel, wretched old nightingale, plucked of its plumage, singing itself hoarse throughout the ages in every tongue, knowing everything, doing nothing." In the book *Jew Suss,* also called *Power,*—Lion Feuchtwanger writes, "They have nothing but the book [The Torah] to read, and the book binds them together." But the whole theme of the book is to "Praise the Lord and be joyous" . . . So now, the people are living the book instead of continually reading it, and they are laughing as they rush along to the beaches at Haifa and Tel-Aviv and chuckling at the least provocation. And it is about time. For all the laughter, multiplied millions of times, won't make up for the tears that those of their kin before them have shed.

I have not enough religion to say that God has wrought a miracle in Israel, but something extraordinary in courage and determination has been given these people who have been able to squeeze themselves out of the lands of oppression. And the miracle is that they were able to win on the battlefield against the most tremendous odds ever heard of in the history of warfare, and that these Jews, from the ages of eight to eighty, have taken mile by mile of barren land and made it blossom. The distance between Israel ground and the Arab lands is about ten feet of no-man's land, like two stage sets set up next to each other: one with trees and fruits and buildings, the other flat desert, as barren as it was five thousand years ago.

And the kids look so strong and healthy and happy, working along with their fathers and mothers and uncles and aunts, completely oblivious of the fact that some of their kin can still smell the gas in the chambers of Dachau and Buchenwald.

The Holy Book is still there and is read on the Sabbath and the holy days; but the people in Israel have found their final salvation in hard work as well as play, and through freedom more so than through reading.

Temptation for me to fool around with words is very strong, and one night in Haifa I made this note on passing a motion picture theater, where there was a line three blocks long waiting to get in: "The book that is to see them through from Here to Eternity is home on the shelf, and they are standing in line to buy tickets to see *From Here to Eternity* in the movie houses." And when you see them come out and say good night to each other, they are not saying, as they did throughout more than two thousand years, "Next year in Jerusalem . . ." I believe if you get close enough, you would hear them say, "Next week, Marilyn Monroe in Cinemascope . . ."

Yes, regardless of the lack of a few American niceties and some small confusion between the old thought and the new, it is my belief that if Israel can continue its great strides in building a nation, it will soon offer an important contribution to the democratic world from a standpoint of culture, production, and a touch of the spiritual—all this, of course, if it is not attacked—and we, in our time, will see a people with a government that follows the thinking of the United States attain greatness. If, however, little Israel is attacked by forces outnumbering it fifty to one or more, we in our time will see many of its attackers dead because of a few feudal lords and a few oil-blinded statesmen who did not want civilization and progress and democracy in the Middle East.

But I believe this will not come to pass and Israel will be in a small measure like these, our blessed United States of America, where men live, as was written in Micah, ". . . and each man shall sit under his own fig tree and none shall make him afraid."

Dear daughter, while you are well mannered and your mother has taught you never to be forward (as of 3:00 p.m., Pacific time, November 12, 1954) I am also glad that you are not timid and that you are ready to speak publicly when an occasion presents itself.

You recall that benefit in Palm Springs, when so many of the stars wanted to go on late in the program, and I sent you on first to make a speech introducing me. You were about eight, but you walked on with the confidence of Sophie Tucker.

However, confidence and assurance wane like anything as we grow older, and you will find when you start thinking of making a graduation speech (which I hope you will do soon) that you will have to be prepared well in your mind before you get up to talk. So, the following is my piece on public speaking.

11. Accustomed As I Am

I HAVE BEEN ASKED hundreds of times to write pieces and even books on public speaking, and this because I have made more speeches at functions of all sorts than anybody I can remember. I have not had the time to write a book of instructions on public speaking, and besides I don't feel it would do much good. The only practical advice would be as follows:

Prepare your speech either in manuscript or notes—notes particularly for the beginner—and be sure you have an opening and a closing: something to get up with and something to sit down with.

Make sure you listen to the other speeches so that you do not repeat the thoughts of the speakers in front of you, as in almost every occasion, the same ideas come to many minds.

And of course the most important thing about addressing the people is a sense of authority—some people have it, some just don't have it, and others can only acquire it through experience and success.

Some years ago, at an inaugural dinner of Mr. Roosevelt's, Earl Wilson of the New York *Post* gave me the title "Toastmaster General of the United States." Right after that Mr. Truman presented me at a White House dinner and said he was pleased to call me what Mr. Wilson had. I have been introduced in this manner ever since. But it is not such a high compliment when you consider that there are so few after-dinner speakers or public orators in show business, and the high compliment to me feels sometimes like a fellow being pointed out as being the greatest violinist in town but that is because he is the only violinist in town.

The radio and television are responsible for the dearth of men who are able to get up on their feet and speak. You can't learn this—may I say art—without having a chance to perfect it. The early radio advertisers continually warned the comedians about being down to earth, as well as the larger motion picture vaudeville houses. Even beginning with "Ladies and Gentlemen" was a little too highbrow. "Hello, folks" and "Hi, kids" was what they wanted, and any three-syllable word was taboo. And because of the rapid strides made by young actors in radio and television, few have ever had the time to read a book or two that might help their vocabulary.

When I first went on the stage, the art of letter-writing was still something to be sought after. The beauty in forming words was a highly desirable gift in writing a letter, and particularly in public speaking. Most people of the theater were well versed in the budgeting of verbiage. In so many plays on Broadway and throughout the country the audiences looked forward to the end of the last act, when the star would come before the curtain, step out of character, and address the audience in what was called "the curtain speech." And these men spoke with great charm and humor, quoting from Shakespeare or translating a phrase from the Latin, as well as speaking of things current in the nation and the world. They were minstrels, if you wish, but gentlemen, if you please.

There were many in the theater who spoke well: Raymond Hitchcock, Francis Wilson, Nat C. Goodwin, Wilton Lackaye, Louis Mann, Henry Miller, De Wolf Hopper, Willie Collier, Richard Bennett, and actually fifty to a hundred more. Today, I don't believe there are ten men, if that many, in the entire amusement business who can make a good speech. Of the newcomers, particularly in radio and TV, I don't think there are three who can get up and open their mouths and make sense. It is not quite all the fault of the newcomers. I don't think anyone awakens in the morning and makes a mental note to be illiterate for the rest of the day. But when a young comic jumps from a borsch circuit salary of fifty dollars a week to three or four thousand a few weeks later, and is then told he can hire six to eight joke-writers, there seems to be something about this kind of a business that stops these fellows from developing their minds.

For a long time I used to begin all my speeches with, "This is an evening to remember and a memory to conjure with"—or marry some fable of Greek mythology to the talents of a buck dancer. And the young radio TV stars around me would look at me as though I were a professor at Ox-

ford. Poor me, from the Bronx, who went to school for a
minute.

At a theatrical dinner lately, in throwing a posy at the
greatest of our contemporary talents, Danny Kaye, I said,
"Not since the original Daniel has a Jew been so lionized,"
and there were at least four TV comedians, each getting
five thousand dollars a week or more who had no idea of
what I was saying.

In movieland, Ronald Reagan and Pat O'Brien speak beautifully and, if you will allow me, Pat thanks me for giving
him the urge. He said it came to him because of an introduction he heard me make a long time ago in presenting the
great Irish tenor, John McCormack, and I think it went
something like this: "It is said of him that when, as a boy,
he sang in the hills of Killarney, the larks hung their heads
for shame." O'Brien liked that.

Since I began speaking at functions at the White House
(not during the Republic Administrations) I have put
every word of my speeches on paper, because the first time
I spoke at a function in Washington, which was arranged
for me by the New York columnist Leonard Lyons (he had
told F.D.R. that I would make him laugh) I came to the
Capitol and was asked to send my speech in that it might
be read to be sure that it would offend no one. Up to that
time I had never put a speech entirely on paper; sometimes
I used only a few notes and sometimes none at all. Since
then, because of making four or five speeches a week on various subjects, I prepare them well in advance and write every
line, and even some gags that sound completely impromptu.
Of course my speeches do not sound like I am reading them,
because it has been my business all my life not to make
them sound so.

Jeri dear, here are some dinners given by the Friars of New York and California to Jack Benny and me, he and I alternating like so: Jack being Toastmaster at my dinner, and I at his.

You will note the style, method of delivery, and the choice of language used by a lot of gentlemen who are, praise the Lord, still with us, and in the public eye, and a few who are not.

I am also including a lecture I delivered in 1950, —most of which was published in the New York Times—militantly attacking the books written in the last few years by Sholom Asch; a speech at the Lambs' Club Dinner; a speech in Hollywood in honor of Sir Laurence and Lady (Vivien Leigh) Olivier; and maybe one or two others, unless the publisher thinks they should be cut out.

12. Testimonial Dinner for George Jessel

TOASTMASTER: JACK BENNY

Clinical Note:
Jack Benny has more ease when speaking at a dinner than any of his contemporaries. First, he is always well prepared and has tried out most of his gags for his staff and his smart wife. His method is that he is never punching too hard, so that should some of his lines fall without laughter, you never hear the thud. Added to this, he has a gentleness that no matter what he says, it never offends anyone. Also, you can tell by what he says that he likes everybody. I never heard him say an unkind word in private or before the public. (Also, there is not much reason for

him to be mad at anyone. He looks twenty years younger than he is, has a fine, healthy family, and several million dollars. So who should he be mad at?)

Jack Benny: Brother Friars, ladies and gentlemen: Unaccustomed as I am to speaking ahead of our guest of honor——I am going to tell you, which you may or not believe, but Jessel did everything in his power to take this job away from me tonight. He wanted to be the guest of honor *and* the Toastmaster——but fortunately, ladies and gentlemen, I happen to be an officer of the Friars' Club, and I put a stop to it. I am the Proctor of the Friars. I was elected Proctor about three months ago. The Proctor of the Friars is equivalent to a photographer on the *Reader's Digest.*—— Just the same, ladies and gentlemen, I am highly flattered that I was asked by our club to be Toastmaster for a dinner given to the greatest Toastmaster in America.—— I mean, it gives me a feeling, even though it may be temporary, that at least I am next best—and being next best to Jessel, whether it is toastmaster, producer, entertainer, or any of his other accomplishments, is quite an achievement.—— Georgie Jessel, I believe, ladies and gentlemen, is the most amazing figure that we have in show business. He is as witty as Groucho Marx, as colorful as Orson Welles, he's as glib of tongue as Bob Hope—and at times he is funnier than Jack Warner. I'll even go further than that. Georgie Jessel is as sophisticated as Noel Coward, as charming as Chevalier, and as versatile as Governor Folsom of Alabama. Mr. Jessel also has the unique distinction of being the only American mentioned in *Who's Who* and the Kinsey Report. Being Toastmaster means that I'll have to jump up here every few minutes—I'll have to be up here all night, so I am not going to take up any more of your time at this moment. If you look up at the dais, you will see what a grand array of speakers we have—the finest dais that I've ever seen. I know that if these gentlemen were paid, it would cost one hundred or two hundred thousand dollars for their performances. Even I have cut my regular fee in half. But in introducing the first speaker tonight, I want to say that every Potash has his Perlmutter. Of course, Jessel would elevate that phrase; he would say every Damon has his Pythias—you know he would make it that high-class. I am sticking to mine, that every Potash has his Perlmutter . . . Hope has his Crosby, I have Fred Allen, Orson Welles has—Orson Welles, and Jessel has Eddie Cantor.

Here's an excerpt of speech made by Eddie Cantor:

Clinical Note:
Cantor is a most forceful speaker. He was the first star of great magnitude to step into social problems. He has spoken for every good cause. When it comes to making a pitch for contributions, there is no one like him. Apropos is a story of how he can make people give that I told at the Press Club in San Francisco:

"Once upon a time, in a little village, there was a group in the market place, talking of strong men. One, to show his prowess, took an orange, squeezed it to nothingness in one movement, and got a glass of orange juice. Then, Cantor took what was left of the orange, and he squeezed it, got two quarts of orange juice and sixty dollars in cash."

Eddie Cantor: It is about time that the Friars honored their Abbot. It is about time that we recognized the greatest after-dinner speaker in this or any other country. It is about time that we brought as the guest of honor, a man whose talents are unparalleled in show business. These, ladies and gentlemen, are not my words. This is taken from the minutes of the meeting at the Friars of March the ninth—and I would like to read it: Subject—*Jessel*, quote: "It is about time that the Friars honored their Abbot. Why do I have to keep making up jokes for Bob Hope and Jack Benny and Al Jolson? (This is still Jessel.) What am I? The Abbot with the Friars or the Abbott with Costello?" And so, on March the tenth, it was unanimously agreed that the Abbot would be given a dinner here, on this night, at the Biltmore Bowl. Ladies and gentlemen, I have known Jessel for a lifetime. I played with George Jessel in the Kid Cabaret of Gus Edwards' of sainted memory,—in 1911. Jessel at that time was thirteen years—not yet thirteen; and so, being of the Jewish faith, he studied diligently for his confirmation—Bar Mitzvah if you will. And the morning of his Bar Mitzvah, he called me on the phone, and he said, "Eddie, today I want you to bring a high hat and a frock coat and striped trousers." I said, "Jessel, that is a funny outfit for me for Bar Mitzvah," and he said, "I am also getting married." Married—little did I know that it was going to become a habit. And so, for thirty-seven years, Georgie Jessel and I have been intimate friends. We have basked in this great warmth we call show business. And Jessel and I have a great deal in common. We have the same temperaments, we have lived the same kind of a life. With us both, it has been one girl after another—and I have paid for mine; as a matter of fact, I paid for some of his!— And he has come a long way in show business. Jack has told you that he is the greatest Toastmaster ever. He is a great comedian, and a producer—but did you ever catch him at a funeral? He is wonderful—most wonderful. These things are nothing for Jessel—he loves to go to a funeral. And all through the years he makes notes on all his friends, because he is a busy man—he wants to be ready. And many times he has called me on the phone. I said, "Hello," and he hung up. He is just checking on my health.——

Here's an excerpt of the speech made by Sam Goldwyn, the distinguished motion picture producer:

Clinical Note:
There are oodles of gags about Mr. Goldwyn, such as his malaprops, like: "I can tell you in two words—'im-possible'!" But Goldwyn, on his feet, always makes sense, and what he means comes through. Sometimes he has a little accent with it, but that goes for Einstein, too, who is also not a "schlemiel"!

Samuel Goldwyn: Governor, Your Honor the Mayor, ladies and gentlemen, and Brother Friars: Before, a little while ago, I had a couple of gags and I tried them out on Bob Hope, and he said, "You are supposed to be a producer, not be funny, and don't try it." So, I am not going to try it and be funny. . . . I wanted to sit at this distinguished table for two specific reasons, first to pay my tribute to the show business ambassador of the world. And second, you don't know what a novelty it is for me to sit and listen to Hope, Cantor, and Kaye speak dialogue that I don't have to pay for.

It is a great satisfaction to me to be able to pay tribute to a man who has been a credit to the show business for so long—and believe me, Georgie has been in business a long, long time. As a matter of fact, he has been in it so long that there are some people that say that Jessel was the actor that shot Lincoln, but I know that couldn't be true. If Lincoln had ever heard Jessel sing, he'd have shot him first. But even if you have any doubts about that Lincoln business, it is a fact that Georgie was tied in closely with another president. As a matter of fact, he was the advance man for Woodrow Wilson. I mean the picture. He made so many speeches for Wilson and Darryl Zanuck, you would have thought that Darryl was running for vice-president.

Here's an excerpt of the speech made by George Burns, of Burns and Allen:

> *Clinical Note:*
> George Burns is my theatrical godson. I met him when he was a humble song-and-dance man, a long time ago, and would turn pale at the thought of adding a new line of dialogue to his vaudeville act. But as soon as he came off the stage and reached the hotel lobby, he had the confidence of General George Patton, Sophie Tucker, and the New York Giants.
> I persuaded him that what he said to a few could be said to the many, and now he has become one of the wittiest speakers of our time. As he talks, stopping to puff a cigar while supposedly thinking of what he will say next (all of which he has already rehearsed for hours in the Men's Room), his pauses and his timing make a snicker turn into a belly laugh. One of his biggest laughs was at a dinner to Judy Garland in which he said, "Judy Garland was very fortunate in having been discovered by Louis B. Mayer when she was ten years old. That could never have happened to me, because when I was ten years old, Louis B. was ten years old."

George Burns: Asking me to talk about Jessel tonight is kind of silly. I have been telling Jessel stories for thirty years. Of course, never in front of a mixed audience. But a guy that has lived as long as Jessel, I am sure that there must be a few clean things that I can think about. Let's see. This is kind of cute. This is years ago. He was playing in Cleveland, and he was doing *The Jazz Singer*, starring in the play. That was before Jolson made it for the Warner Brothers. And incidentally, there is a great story that goes with that *Jazz Singer* deal. You see, Jessel starred in the play and felt this was his property, so when Warner Brothers signed Jolson it burned him up, and he took an oath that he would break Warner Brothers and Al Jolson if it cost him his last cent. And he will do it, too! The fact of the matter is it is only a matter of days when Jolson and Warner Brothers will be broke, because Jessel is down to his last eighteen dollars. But anyway, let's go back to what happened in Cleveland. Jessel was starring in the play *The Jazz Singer*, and I was playing one of the outlying houses. At the time there was a girl in town giving lectures on psychology, and Jessel invited me to supper after the show, and I went over there—the Statler Hotel—went up to Jessel's room, and this girl was there. And about two o'clock in the morning, Jessel—er-er . . . no, I am wrong. I can't tell this in front of a mixed audience.—— But later on, I will be glad to tell it to you ladies alone.

But I am sure that there must be some clean thing that I can think about that I can tell everybody. Oh yes, Jessel was playing in San Francisco, and Eddie Cantor got a wire that Jessel was very sick—and Cantor flew up there with a doctor. In the meantime there was a Chinese girl on the bill that came into Jessel's dressing room to find out how Georgie was feeling, and at the same moment the doctor and Cantor walked in. I can't tell this one either . . . Jessel was booked on the

Orpheum Circuit, and he was playing Winnipeg, and on the bill was an act called Crovney and Brown Acrobatic Dancers . . . And this Crovney was the most beautiful girl you have ever seen. Great contortionist. And in Winnipeg, it gets very cold. So, Jessel— From there he played Vancouver. And in Vancouver, he was on the bill with a big act called Lasky's Redheads, and there was a tall girl called Elsie Huber, and after rehearsal— Then he went to Seattle. In Seattle there was a restaurant right alongside of the theater, and there was a blond waitress . . . In Portland.—— Well, anyway this is silly. There must be something I can say about Jessel. I owe a lot to him, and I love him.

Here's an excerpt of the speech of Bob Hope:

Clinical Note:

Hope is faster on his feet than anybody. The gags come like next year's machine gun, and when some of his lines don't get laughs, he always has something to save them, like: "This sounded awfully funny in my room," or, "When a writer gets old, you got to fire him. In my business you can't be sentimental."

Bob Hope: I want to tell you that I think it is wonderful, ladies and gentlemen, to give this Twentieth-century producer and Nineteenth-century vaudevillian a dinner. I saw his latest picture, *Nightmare Alley*—I liked it. Out at Twentieth Century, anybody is a producer who can handle a croquet mallet—but that is not true of Georgie. Georgie is a key man out there. He is a key man: every time Zanuck goes to the washroom, Jessel hands him the key. But he is a wonderful guy—he really is—and from the start of Georgie's career, you knew that he was destined for greatness. It was obvious that nothing could stop him—not even his talent. Just take a look at him: forty years in show business. He has not a gray hair in his head—well, he didn't have this afternoon. He is so versatile, even his hair changes moods. He is a wonderful fellow, he really is. Forty years old and he is the youngest of the Cantor-Jolson-Jessel trio. He has been in the business forty years, and he is the youngest. Before him, it was Cantor-Jolson and Shakespeare. But I could really stand up here and say a lot of things about Georgie—just from hearsay. George Burns told you nothing about him—but he is—he has had quite a career, this man who is sometimes referred to as the Anthony Eden of Pico Boulevard——the Kosher Errol Flynn. But one thing we all admit is that he is a great sentimentalist. We know him as the male Sophie Tucker. Ladies and gentlemen, he really is a great sentimentalist, and he cried like a baby the other day when Truman made that speech about the draft. Georgie thought they were taking girls from eighteen to twenty-five. And it is a funny thing—I know him pretty well, and I know that he doesn't give a second thought to women. His first thought covers everything. And I am happy to report tonight that he does not chase women as much as he used to. He had his desk sawed in half so that he can take a short cut. . . . He is a wonderful guy—and he is a very loyal fellow. He is crazy about his boss, Zanuck. The other night at the Academy Awards when Darryl bent over to kiss the Oscar, Jessel bent over to kiss Zanuck. It was a pretty sight. I can't tell you what he does to keep his job, but it is banned in Boston. And he has great talent. Of course, we can't forget that

Georgie sings, too. A lot of people tried . . . but it is not true he is the original voice of the turtle.

Here's an excerpt of the speech made by Al Jolson:

> *Clinical Note:*
> Al was never much of a speaker, and it never worried him, because he always brought his piano players, Harry Akst and Martin Freed; and after a few lines, he would break into a song, or maybe a dozen! And though he insisted on being the last to go on at every function, as he did in the theater, he would always complain to the audience that he begged to go on earlier but they wouldn't let him do it.

Al Jolson: Tonight you are looking at the goose who is going to lay the golden egg. Why I am brought at this ungodly hour to tell jokes or to make any speech, I don't know. I have not any speech, I haven't any writers to write me jokes, but I am proud of one thing—that I am standing up here, and I am able to say things about Jessel. Of course, I resent that crack Mr. Benny made about me having five million dollars . . . I have seven . . . and I'll need it—because after tonight nobody will want me. But I want to pay tribute to Jessel, and why he tried to sing like me for thirty years, and always was flat, I'll never know—so now I'm going to imitate him. (Mr. Jolson then sang "My Mother's Eyes" kidding me and several other songs, and had he wanted to, he could have sung all night.)

My speech, after receiving the Friars' Medal of Honor, was as follows:

George Jessel: This has been a most trying evening for me, listening to many gentlemen highly successful in their own vocations, attempting to be after-dinner speakers. Considering this great fund of inexperience, they have done remarkably well, and I compliment them, as I would compliment a sixty-year-old baseball umpire who had crocheted a fine lace tablecloth. Most men who are recipients of testimonial dinners such as this are immediately overcome with emotion when called to their feet, and they generally begin a hesitant address by saying, "Oh, my friends, I have no words for this . . ." I have more words than in *Gone with the Wind.* And as to the phrases and the many shafts that have been wafted at me by some of the speakers, it would be nice if I were overcome by the close proximity of these celebrated people. Unfortunately I am not. I don't think that posterity will be as generous as you have been with your laughter and applause to most of the speakers. Look through your mind's eye and see what might be written of most of them in the future—a short word-portrait of their careers: Mr. Cantor, favorite radio star of the Crystal Set day—Mr. George Burns, whose life-line of existence is depending on what Gracie will say when he says, "—and then what happened to your brother??" Mr. Danny Kaye, current favorite of a shattered and bankrupt Great Britain—Mr. Bob Hope, the most popular comedian of an era when America was in its most bewildered state—Mr. Pat O'Brien, a Vine Street Parnell—Mr. Jolson, with a great success shielded from the public eye by a handsome boy in his twenties and a thousand fat Victor records. And the Toastmaster —every schmuck is a Toastmaster. I am not particularly gratified when complimented by so many insinuations that it is about time that honor was paid to me.

I am glad the young lady with whom I have a date

later in the evening is here to hear these nice things about me; but there's much more I'd like her to hear about me. As a child I made up many sayings which are known the world over: "A friend in need is a friend indeed" is one of them. Another: "Money you make like that will never do you any good." "Rockefeller can only wear one suit at a time," was one of my phrases,—and I should have been happy if the preceding speakers had mentioned the help I had been to men throughout the years. I wish I could say this in the second or third person.

I recall working along the waterfront in Albany many years ago, and seeing a young man having trouble starting his boat. I helped him. He never forgot it. That man was Robert Fulton, ladies and gentlemen.

The world does not know this, nor did you hear it from the mouth of the speakers—of how I was called up to Washington by a great man at a time when our country was in great hazard. When he said to me, "Georgie, I don't know what to do about this general I have. He drinks, he smokes, and with his beard people think he looks Jewish; I am being terribly criticized . . ." And I said, "Abe, keep Grant, and let McClellan go . . ." A publisher who lives in San Simeon sent for me some months ago and said to me, "Georgie, I have a man who I feel is right for the presidency, and I want you to help him in public utterance." So, while most of you think I was appearing at the Carnival—a saloon in New York —I was in Loew's Tokyo, ladies and gentlemen. And I helped this man. I said to him, "MacArthur, your speeches are too flowery—you sound as if you have a Godhead complex. The public don't want that. Remember you are just a man, Doug—you aren't Zanuck." Not only have I helped my fellow men, but I have helped dumb animals as well. Some years ago I met a horse as a two-year-old and nobody wanted to bet on him . . . a thin, skinny horse, Rosenberg was his name. I made him change his name to Rosemont, and he won at the Santa Anita Handicap.

But all this is yesterday's roses—all this is klabriash in a tunnel. More than anyone else, I think, in America, do I know how much bunkum there is in testimonial dinners. I have had, through my years in public life, to tell more lies about guests-of-honor than any one of my contemporaries. I have screamed their virtues from the speaker's table, hiding their vices in my own conscience. But I've found this to be true—I have never known anyone who was the recipient of a testimonial dinner who did not have something that was pretty good—some slight decent quality. No one ever gave a dinner for Lefty Louie or Sittin' Bull—and so, after forty years in show business, I am inclined to look at things philosophically. I don't know whether or not life begins at forty. If it does, it begins from the neck up. For the manuscript of life is a tragi-farce, there is very little mystery in it. And we know very soon the finish and we reach for our hats and our hearts. At this moment the scene is light and gay, and for me completely is the manuscript sweetly scented. As the curtain rises, I find myself at this moment basking on the right side of the stage. I am not a rich man, but at this milestone in a minstrel's career I find myself blessed with good health and a little daughter who gives every sign of being a comfort to me in the twilight years. And I am further blessed having so many acquaintances and friends, not only here but throughout all America—but particularly these who have come tonight to break bread in this intimate scene with me. And as for myself and the manuscript, I find the part that I play is a good part, for I play a man with many faults, who makes many mistakes and many, many speeches. It is natural that a man pause at this stage of his life and think of those of close kinship that we want with us only at moments of compliment. And as I say that, because by force of being middle-aged and sentimental, my eyes fill up—and this is a cue to end my speech—and I take it—and like so, I salute the distinguished gentlemen who have said words in praise—and like so, I throw a kiss to you assembled—and like so, I sit down.

*Jeri, you have asked me to come to your school
and speak to the class about the art of being a Toastmaster.*

*I think that whatever lessons I could teach would
have a better effect on paper, so here's a series of
introductions of several important people that made
for a very successful evening. The words are carefully
budgeted, the introductions have been carefully
guarded against repetition, and it is the best I have to
offer to those who would stand and talk.*

13. Dinner for Jack Benny

TOASTMASTER: GEORGE JESSEL

BROTHER FRIARS, His Honor the Mayor of the
City of New York, His Excellency the Governor of Illinois,
the state in which this frugal incident was born, Ladies and
Gentlemen:

The way is long from whence I came, and the shrine is far
where I yearn to be, yet I have left the weight of business at
my producer's desk in Hollywood to speak at this occasion.

It is only within the year that I have stood at this speaker's
pulpit and as Friar Laurence says in *Romeo and Juliet:* "St.
Francis, be my steed for oft have I stumbled over these
graves before!" And thus is the life of a public talker. Year
after year I find myself telling lie after lie, covering the frail-
ties of men with compliments, finding virtue where none exists, and tossing rare orchids at the faces of men whose faces

should be covered with *tzimmis*. (A Middle East dish of prunes and carrots.)

And this year, working with the sovereign state of California, I have functioned at every known affair that was given. I have run the gamut. I have spoken the same day at the launching of a destroyer at the harbor of San Pedro, and at a circumcision in Glendale. And fortunately I was able to use the same speech at both occasions.

Now, ladies and gentlemen, at almost every affair, the Toastmaster's plate and his chair are the recipient of many telegrams from well-wishers who did not buy a ticket but sent a telegram, and thereby perforce of sending a telegram they imagine that their names will be read, and it might be a commercial for their businesses; such as *Wish I could be with you tonight in honor of Jack Benny—Zelocopsky's Furniture Store, 426 Linwood Avenue, Newark, New Jersey.* These telegrams I tear up.——

And then, again, we have two that are worthy of reading, and very definitely worthy because it marks the most important moment in the career of a minstrel who needs no money or needs nothing to give him any further kudos. This is a telegram that says: *All the men in service in the Far East Command, and the women, too, send you their warm-hearted greetings and equally warm-hearted best wishes. They will be ever grateful for your selfless and patriotic service to them.—M. R. Ridgway, General, U. S. Army.* And the other, from a man who is sometimes challenged because he does not send telegrams, but writes letters—the most important American of this time, and the president of the greatest country the world has ever known. And he says very warmly: *All good wishes to you and Mary on this occasion of your twentieth anniversary on the radio.—Harry S. Truman.*

And so, with all this, this evening is indeed one to remember and a memory to conjure with. (I also used this phrase at the battleship launching and at the circumcision.) For the guest of honor, this evening, is a man about whom it is most easy to hurl superlatives, for not only the younger generation, but also it is easy for older showmen and troupers like myself to sing his praises. For I am not one of those who have refused to emerge from their own particular capsule of time, who have lived their lives continually repeating to themselves. "Kid McCoy could have licked Marciano—Mathewson was better than Bob Feller—King Solomon was smarter than B. M. Baruch," and all these bromidic phrases are of the same category as the attempt in consoling a man who is carrying a torch for a loved one and the well-meaning friends say, "There are other fish in the sea"; "There's a rose on every bush"; and "Never chase a streetcar, there'll be another along in a minute."

Also, there are too many older men who live in the past and who stay married to yesterday, who believe there is only charm in what can never return.

No, I believe that Jack Benny would have held his own at any time in the history of the American theater. I don't say that he would have been mentioned in the same aura as Richard Mansfield, Henry Irving, and Otis Skinner—and I don't think he would have been talked about in the same milieu with Warfield, Sam Bernard, Hitchcock, Eddie Foy— and I don't think people would have put him in the same class as Frank Tinney, W. C. Fields, Willie Collier—but I do think he would have held his own with Harry "Zoop" Welsh, "Sliding Billy" Watson, "Billy, the Tramp," Arlington or Lou "Wow, here comes a woman" Fink.

And, therefore, since he has served the people well in twenty years on the radio, and now since he has gone on even to further success in the newest of the arts—you should excuse the expression—television, we find ourselves under these most happy circumstances of breaking bread in his honor. And for that reason there have come from all corners of our country, a group of distinguished gentlemen to toast him for the past and applaud him for the future.

INTRO: MAYOR IMPELLITERI

Foremost among these and the first speaker of the evening will be His Honor, the Mayor, and then other comedians will follow. I have had the privilege and the honor to know the present chief magistrate of the city before this evening and, echoing the votes of the majority of New Yorkers, I can rightly sing his praises. He has kept his promises—and that is a strange thing in the world of politics—for the promises of men in political life are likened to the robes of the Princess Penelope in Greek mythology—they are woven in the morning, unraveled at night. (Aside: This is a line from *David and Bathsheba* or from something).

And now with the hope of more jesting to follow and with profundity the order of the moment, I am very proud of the opportunity to bring to this speaker's pulpit, His Honor, the Mayor of New York . . . *Vincent Impelliteri.*

INTRO: WILLIAM S. PALEY

The next speaker is one of the two great presidents and heads of the world's foremost broadcasting chains. There are some men who are to the amusement world born. There are some who should have never been born at all. But it seems to me that this handsome young man, who is actually about the same age that the guest of honor lies about, has gone further in his short space of time than almost any other American. And his entree into the radio world was also in a very direct way, for it stems actually from the theater. In the long ago, his beloved dad and grandfather lived in Philadelphia and were inveterate theatergoers. They never guessed that years later their son and grandson would provide entertainment for nothing. They happily paid for their seats in the Chestnut Street Opera House, and they were particularly intrigued by a play called *Mrs. Wiggs of the Cabbage Patch.* Night after night they came to see *Mrs. Wiggs of the Cabbage Patch*—and after watching and being emotionally stirred by the scene in which Mrs. Wiggs picked the cabbage, they decided to manufacture the "La Palina" cigar. It was from this cabbage that the next speaker was enabled to go to college and it was the great desire to get away from this cabbage that prompted him to enter a new field that he alone among his associates saw the great future in—and so he built a great industry, because of his personal contribution, his integrity, and his warm personality. Even NBC spelled backwards is CBS. I am very happy to present to you *Mr. William S. Paley.*

INTRO: FRED ALLEN

The next speaker is an old friend of the American public, an old friend of mine, and regardless of any contrived feuds he has had with the guest of honor, they are great friends. He is one of the strangest men in the amusement world. But because of his great wit and his personal goodness, he can be allowed whatever idiosyncrasies he is said to have. The beginning of his career is a romantic one. As a little boy in Boston, he acted in the mob scenes of a play called *Kismet*—the Arabic word for "fate"—and the principle character of this play is a man called Hajji, a juggler, and the symbolic impact of the character in the play is: "We are all pawns in the hands of Fate, who keeps the balls leaping from his hands willy-nilly without knowing or caring which one will fall to the ground."

I am sure this old philosophy had its effect on the little boy who will soon speak to you, for he immediately set out upon a career as a juggler. His name was not the one we all know him by—his right name was John Sullivan—that evidently sounded too Jewish, so he changed it. He has served in almost all the branches of the amusement tree, and has served them well. I never believed this supposed feud that the gullible public swallowed—that he and the guest of honor are on bad terms. What could they have argued about? It certainly wasn't the money! And it surely couldn't have been about sex, because the only reference to sex that Fred ever had on his program was when "Howdy Bub" said he had a cow with a nice big tail. And so, with no more jokes after which I might seem pale by comparison, I bring you one of the great humorists of these—our contemporary times—*Fred Allen.*

Note: This is one of the very few appearances made by Fred Allen, and probably only the second or third after-dinner speech in his career—and he was an absolute riot. He had worked hard and prepared one of his inimitable monologues, and they screamed at him. When his applause had finally subsided, I arose and said, "I had intended to tell a joke right here, but after Mr. Allen's speech, good showman that I am, I'll recite Lincoln's Gettysburg Address."

INTRO: GOVERNOR ADLAI E. STEVENSON OF ILLINOIS

And now from the juggler of wit to a man of great responsibility who cannot let men be pawns of Fate like the juggler, but has to look after the welfare of millions of Americans in his great state—and I might add, that since he has been in office in his particular state, its city of Chicago has fared much better in the public eye than in the years before. If ever a city has been censored too much, it has been the city of Chicago. Some years ago I remember playing at the Sam Harris Theatre, and on Randolph Street close by, a little boy fell off his bicycle and tore his overalls. The little boy was unhurt and was laughing, and he had other overalls at home. The newspapers throughout America printed the incident in headlines as follows: CHILD MORTALLY INJURED AS GUNMEN WRECK THE LOOP WITH MACHINE GUN BULLETS. Yes, most of the things said about Chicago are all embellished lies—like me with girls!

And so I have an extreme warm feeling in presenting this distinguished gentleman to you because he is a great Democrat.

Ladies and gentlemen, his Excellency, the Governor of the sovereign State of Illinois, *Governor Adlai E. Stevenson.*

Note: When Governor Stevenson finished (incidentally, this is the first time Broadway had ever heard him speak), he was on his feet just two or three minutes, but he was great. I started to tell a gag after his applause was over, and suddenly noticed the audience of more than fifteen hundred turning their heads to the right, and then applause started until it came out like thunder, for Bernard M. Baruch had come in late and was making his way to the speakers' table. I naturally stopped speaking when Baruch arrived but, from the side of my mouth, I said *sotto voce;* but so that the audience could hear, "If you were not such a great guy, I would give you hell for walking in right in the middle of the gag I was telling."

INTRO: GEORGE BURNS

And now I shall bring to this speakers' podium another straight man and the luckiest straight man who ever lived. From his lips alone shall we hear the truth about the guest of honor. They have spent years together behind the warm curtain in the lost art of vaudeville. I stress the word "vaudeville" because I doubt if the next speaker is conversant with anything else. While I don't say that it is necessary for a man to be a student of Shakespeare or Molière, or Racine, or Rostand, I do think that a man in his middle age should know that there is some printed matter besides *Variety*. It is only in the last two decades that one was sure how to present the next speaker, he having had so many different names as a vaudeville actor. He was Bernard of Bernard & Gary; Williams of Brown & the Williams Brothers; Mack of Mack, Albright & Mack; and in the Nagasaki Japanese Troupe, he was known as Abe Stern. After having had so many masculine associates and partners, he felt that if he was to get anywhere in the world of the theater, he had best find for himself a woman partner. And later, when he did so well and started to broaden his earning power, he turned to the Scriptures, wherein he found the proverb, "Man cannot live by bread alone, he must also marry a very clever woman." Then he read again from the Scriptures, wherein a prophet seeing one less fortunate said, "There, but for the grace of God go I"— And so, "there but for the grace of Gracie," a man who would still be Abe Stern of the Nagasaki Japs, I present to you, my beloved friend—*George Burns*.

INTRO: BERNARD M. BARUCH

And now from Abe Stern to the sublime. A man not often seen at public affairs, yet a man called into public affairs when the nation needs him, and in these, our times, this has been necessary so often—and he has always responded. The Toastmaster is fortunate again to have often felt the warmth of his handclasp, and has been fortunate further in knowing his whole family. There are many legends about our next speaker. It is said that America's eldest statesman, as he is aptly called, has never taken a penny for his services (which cannot be said of many statesmen today). There is also a legend about him that his great philosophy comes to him while he sits in Central Park. This, of course, is apropos to stories like *Washington and the Cherry Tree,* etc. I don't believe that his philosophy comes to him because he sits in Central Park—I have an uncle who has been sitting in Mt. Morris Park for thirty years and not only is he not a philosopher but he has been arrested six times for annoying the pigeons.

But the next speaker is a man that the Almighty God has gifted with wisdom and goodness and has rewarded him with many years beyond the threescore and ten—and it is not mere coincidence that his name translated from the Hebrew means "blessed"—and blessed he is indeed. Ladies and gentlemen, *Bernard M. Baruch.*

INTRO: JACK BENNY

Ladies and gentlemen, your Toastmaster has always found it a problem in the budgeting of words when introducing a particular guest of honor that he has known through the years and whom he has loved very dearly. I never was able to hold back and not show my emotion in the past years when I would bring to his feet George M. Cohan or Jimmy Walker—but sometimes when presenting Jim—and I would that his memory be kept ever green in this great city—I would have to hide behind a character and not speak as myself. Once during a campaign I remember presenting him in this manner: by going back to the medieval days and speaking as a herald who, with trumpet in hand, comes to a small hamlet, tells the populace to make way for a high and mighty personage. And so, because out in California I see Jack almost every day, because just a few days ago I lunched, dined, and then appeared on his radio show, and because I am so honestly fond of him, I would like to dismiss myself in the first person and take on the character of a lawyer representing him in court. Thus appearing in his defense, I would say, "Your Honor, ladies and gentlemen of the jury, you, the American public, I wish to say about my client that I have known him throughout the years and, like these witnesses on the stand today, I also vouch for his character. That the record shows that from a most humble beginning, with the help of no one but himself, he must be acquitted of any possible charge that would be brought against him in the amusement business. I ask that the jury must agree with me, that for twenty years he has served the public honestly and he has edited wisely the speeches of himself and the characters on his radio shows, he has never said one thing in twenty years to offend the most sensitive boy, girl, man or woman of his great legion of listeners. He has in times of war left his home and his business to go to the farthest corners of the world to entertain the soldiers of our country. He has only lately taken his life in his hands by bringing good cheer into the very peaks of Heartbreak Ridge in Korea. He has given of his time and his money to every good cause, even when not called upon. He is as good a father and husband as he is a humorist. And I love him with all my heart."

And now, with your permission, Your Honor, the Toastmaster rests his case and I call *Jack Benny* to the stand.

14. Lambs' Club Speech
1948

His Excellency, Governor Warren; his Honor, Mayor Bowron; distinguished fellow players, the Lambs and their Ewes—ladies and gentlemen. May I first thank Major Rupert Hughes for his warm summation of my various virtues. I agree with him. Did I not, 'twould be perjury. As Abbot of the Friars, I am particularly gratified for the opportunity of speaking before this Aryan audience and to bring tribute in words from the Friars to the Lambs.

May I say firstly that this is the happiest picture of a Lambs' Gambol I've seen in some time. The Lambs that have strayed from 44th Street to California make the pasture seem greener than the one between Broadway and Sixth Avenue. This roadside and the earth are more sensitive and therefore softer to rest upon for a minstrel wandering. This I read in a script yesterday.

But believe me to be honestly enjoying the fact that I am here as an actor speaking to an audience of actors. This opportunity doesn't come very often in an age of synthetic amusement, an age where one needs the microphone for every possible use, all this brought about by the radio which John Dos Passos so aptly called "the rape of the elements." And now television, wherein creatures are cut down to the size of little brownies, all looking like they need a shave. Not small enough to be midgets and not large enough to be with the William Morris office. This is the day that we live in. Shades of Southern, Mansfield, Ward & Vokes. Where, oh where has most of the theater gone? *Sic transit* Gloria Swanson.

At the Friars' Club an actor complained that he didn't know anyone. "These people don't talk like actors," he said. Of course he didn't know them. They were not actors. And at the Lambs' Club the last time I was there, there was a sadder scene. I also didn't understand what the men were talking about—and they were actors, and I didn't know them. How different the scene in a more majestic yesterday. A gallery stood around a table listening to a battle of wits between Wilton Lackaye and Augustus Thomas. And in another corner Henry Dixie reminiscing with Francis Wilson and David Warfield. Actors at the bar recalling experiences, romantic moments of plays of the road . . . "remember that week we played in Spokane?" . . . "I was in the *Prince of Pilsen*" . . . "I was with *Captain Jinks of the Horse Marines*" . . . "Remember when we played together in *The Girl from Rectors?*" Compare this with the parley in the Lambs today:

"Well, hello, kid, haven't seen you since we did that commercial for Meyer's Stomach Drops" . . . "Yes, you did. I did the squeaking door on the Ex-lax show with you" . . . "Oh, sure—how's your Trendex rating?" . . . "Swell, how's your Nielsen?" . . . "Fine" . . . "Mine's up an eighth" . . . "Mine's down a quarter" . . . "I'm on at a bad time—five forty-five in the morning singing lullabies for gamblers" . . . "See you tomorrow. I got to rehearse. I'm doing a commercial for the new Chocolate Smear Show."

Ah, sweet memories of yesterday and those who have gone down the road to their fathers. If I may quote from a book of mine . . .

"Where are Joe and Lew, Sam H. and Sam
Bernard, Hitchy, Foy and sweet George M.?

"All are sleeping under the hill, dreaming
of Broadway, and how proud Frohman looked
as he walked into the Empire with Maude
Adams at his side."

I remember so well my first public appearance as an actor.
I was nine years old—over thirty years ago. I was singing on
a street corner in the Bronx. Not me alone. We were a trio.
Myself, Walter Winchell, and Eddie Cantor. What happened to them—this I don't know.

There we were singing "School Days" and a Tammany
politician came by. Malone was his name and he said,
"How'd you kids like to make a dollar tonight?" I said,
"What doing?" He said. "You come down with me to 42nd
Street and Times Square and you sing the song 'Tammany'
and you'll give out election buttons." This was the time
when William J. Gaynor was running for mayor in New
York. Mr. Gaynor was a most distinguished-looking man
with a high silk hat and a long black beard. Evidently he
needed votes from the Times Square section. In the Bronx
they thought he was a rabbi on a vacation and they voted
right away.

And then I remember going home to the house where I
lived with my mother and grandparents, a little Bronx flat
on Simpson Street, to ask my mother if I could go down
and sing late at night on the corner of 42nd Street. It was
a nice place then, the Bronx.

And on the summer nights the parents would keep their
heads out of the windows waiting for their respective daugh-
ters to come home from the many dances that they used to
have in that neighborhood of Fort George and Starlight Park.
Sweet, simple dances. Yet they were conducive to increasing

the population of the Bronx to a great measure. So the parents would lean with their heads out the window to see that when daughter arrived home with the fellow she came right into the house and didn't make any monkey business in the vestibule. Oh, what went on in those vestibules in the Bronx and the things we found in our letter boxes. You know—love notes—Dear Sam, I love you . . . etc.

But anyway I went downtown and sang and then later on we kids went into Childs Restaurant on 43rd Street. That was the rendezvous for a lot of actors. Theater, theater, theater—that's all you heard. Thwarted ambitions—dreams soon to be realized—theater, theater, theater. I remember sitting next to one of those old-fashioned guys with the fur-collared coat. He immediately spouted that he had just returned from thirty-nine weeks with a repertoire company. He had played everything and he said to the waitress, "I would like some peach pie." And she said, "We have no peach pie." And he said, "Fake it—fake it."

And oh the lies he told me. How Mr. Drew and Mr. Southern were taught every move by him. But all this belongs to an old book that for some reason or other has crushed violets between its pages. And my appearances as an actor when away from my desk as a motion picture producer at Twentieth Century-Fox and for which I am very grateful—(and every night I pray to the good Lord that things continue as they are) . . . Anyway my only appearances are sometimes playing an engagement with one of my pictures or making a speech for some cause.

And so—as it was in the beginning of my speech, so shall it be at the end. I love actors and I love the theater. The late and lamented George M. Cohan said a wonderful thing one day. Somebody asked him to join a club whose members were a group of fine businessmen, and George M. said, "Oh no. I couldn't do that. If I joined a club I might take a few drinks, and if I was drinking I wouldn't want anybody to see me but actors. See what I mean? Nobody but actors."

And so—the Abbot of the Friars salutes the Lambs. Long may you gambol! For perhaps it is written that the Friars and the Lambs shall lie down together even if only the agents get up. So here's to fellow players everywhere. To every actor, be he Puck or the Dane Melancholic. And here's to the theater who like Madam Godam in the *Shanghai Gesture* must survive. Come talking pictures, come radio, come television, come all things not of the human flesh, the theater will survive. For it is a temple that will not be destroyed—not even by the Romans. Here's to us—you and I—members of a noble profession. Yes by God—a noble profession.

15. United Jewish Appeal and Bond Drives
1952

I COME TO YOU TO SPEAK about a most important subject to us who are assembled here, to other Americans of the Jewish faith, and to people of all faiths and in all other Democratic countries—but particularly important to us. I have come here to ask you to aid the United Jewish Appeal, which reaches out and in its merciful arms brings aid to Israel. Not only because the inhabitants of this new bulwark of democracy have the same religion that we have been born with, but because in aiding Israel, we are the Marshall Plan of the East, morally, spiritually, and economically. What we do to help through the United Jewish Appeal gives those poor wanderers, who have survived the concentration camps and the crematories, hope and faith. A faith in the Almighty God, that through all the years of persecution, still kindles a fire in almost every Jewish heart.

Mark Twain said, "All things are mortal but the Jew; all other forces pass, but he remains."

Benjamin Disraeli, later Earl of Beaconsfield, said, "The attempt to extirpate the Jew has been made under the most favorable auspices, and on the largest scale and for the longest period of time. Egyptian Pharaohs, Assyrian kings, Roman emperors, Scandinavian crusaders, Gothic princes and Holy Inquisitors have alike devoted their energies to the fulfillment of this common purpose. Expatriation, exile, captivity, confiscation, torture on the most ingenious, and massacre on the most extensive scale, have been tried in vain. The Jew, however, remains!"

But, as against these profound utterances, let me tell you of an incident in San Francisco a few months ago. I went there to go on the television, to stay on all night to help the Saints & Sinners Milk Fund of the great Bay City— and while girding my loins for that long siege, I took a walk in the crisp October air to the older part of the city and there I came upon an old synagogue—its date 1884— and I walked in. The very old sexton was busy cleaning around when I said to him, "May I ask you a question? Is this a newly built building with the date being only the origin of its first building?" He said, "No, it was never changed." I said, "Well, how is it that when you had the great fire in 1906 when everything in this section was destroyed that nothing happened to this building?" He looked at me in amazement, then said, "A synagogue? Are you crazy?"

I know it will not be necessary, particularly to you people, to review the misery and torture that befell the Jewish people throughout Europe when it was under the reign of the devil and the beasts of Berlin. For I am told that the Jewish Federation Drive in your city will reach a goal that will be an increase over last year's generous contributions. And in doubling your energies here in your own city, you have not forgotten, and will not forget, the plight and the needs of your religious brothers overseas.

And now to a few moments of business . . .

Overseas, the need for aid provided by the United Jewish Appeal is as great as ever. The lifesaving job of the UJA must continue. A minimum of one hundred twenty thousand

Jews in Eastern Europe and Arab lands must be moved to Israel this year. As tensions and unrest mount in these danger areas, the need for rescue becomes more acute.

Meanwhile, more than two hundred fifty thousand Jews in Europe and the Moslem world depend upon your assistance for urgently needed clothing, food, medical aid, rehabilitation, and vocational assistance. For five dollars a Jewish child in North Africa can be taken out of the squalor and despair of a *mellah* to enjoy the rare privilege of a week's vacation. And a vacation there means a vacation from hunger, sickness, and gloom. It means a week of sunlight and fresh air, nourishing food and medical treatment.

When you stop to think that since 1948 when the young democracy successfully withstood the invasion of Israel by five Arab armies, Israel's enemies have watched and waited, hoping for her collapse. The Syrian delegate to the United Nations declared, according to a newspaper report, "Israel's economy will soon make her melt away; there will be no need for war to achieve the new state's downfall."

He set the date for the Jewish state's collapse as 1955 when he said, "The United Nations will have to appoint a Jewish commissioner to administer the country, since it would liquidate economically and politically." I think the Syrian delegate will be proven wrong. In fact, I know it! Israel can win this fight if we do our job quickly and thoroughly!

My friends, through the efforts of all of us, we have brought the homeless to Israel, but we dare not, and can not, leave them homeless there. Israel's fate and the success of all our previous efforts, depend on what we do these few years. Then the dream of a free Israel will surely be realized.

During the sad, mad years of Hitlerism I was asked by

B'nai B'rith to write a short piece, the wordage of which might bring hope—and I wrote the following:

TO THOSE IN BONDAGE

Alas, poor Israel, lonely, tired nightingale, singing itself hoarse for two thousand years in every tongue to a multitude of ears who listen unimpressed, and the Star of David grows less brilliant as each night falls. You saw a mirage, Master Moses; you hear only the wishful beating of your heart's desire, Father Abraham, shout four million Jews in the dark ghettos of Europe. And then, from a corner in a shattered synagogue under a window whose glass has been spat upon and broken, comes the voice of a young student. He reads from his book. It is written "Have YE faith, children of Israel, God's delay is not God's denial—have YE faith." And four million Jews lift up their heads and speak the Benediction:

> SHMA ISRAEL . . . ADENOY ELEHENU . . .
> ADENOY EH CHOD

> HEAR, OH ISRAEL . . . THE LORD OUR GOD
> . . . THE LORD IS ONE.

And the weak once again are strong.

Most American Jews don't look into their past far enough. They see only as far back as a generation of immigrants landing at Ellis Island and Castle Garden . . . Men and women and children marked by lines of misery from oppression abroad, speaking in dialects, carrying packs on their backs, eating the simple food of Eastern European peasantry—the *luckshon,* the carrots, the raw onions . . . shrinking into alley ways at the sight of policemen, still with fear in their hearts of the Cossacks and the Prussian Hussars. And that is as far as some modern American Jew looks back.

Let them look back farther and farther, and their chests will fill out, and their heads will rise in pride, and their hearts will beat with joy, for they will find that their fathers, and their fathers before them, were people who brought Godliness to the entire world—that they wrote the eternal page on which all civilization is founded—The Ten Commandments. That they were the authors of all that is good in Christianity—that the Jews brought more morality and spirituality to mankind than all of the other people of the world put together.

All these things you may say belong to the past. Then I would tell you to look upon the handful of people who are the new state of Israel. Heroes all, with the courage of the Maccabees of old, but not old Patriarchs with long beards and prayers, young modern, skilled men and women and children, fighting for their existence—and maybe for yours and mine—and for their faith in Almighty God.

16. Hollywood Welcomes
Sir Laurence and Lady Olivier

FROM THE HOLLYWOOD *Reporter*

Mr. AND MRS. DANNY KAYE were the hosts to a welcome party to Sir Laurence Olivier and Lady Olivier (Vivien Leigh) given at the Crystal Room of the Beverly Hills Hotel to the four hundred of the motion picture colony. The evening's highlight was a piece of character acting by George Jessel.

Kaye introduced Mr. Jessel in this manner: "We are fortunate in having the oldest living actor with us tonight—George Glenweather Krelby."

Jessel came on wearing a cape, holding a gold cane, and aided by two men almost carrying him to the microphone.

His speech follows.

Ladies and gentlemen, I am at a great disadvantage to be called out of my bed at midnight to make a speech in honor of this young song-and-dance man, Lawrence Tierney.

However, I've made a few notes—(from under his Inverness cape he took out six or seven large manuscripts, glanced through them, and tore out one page, then coughed for three minutes and continued).

Ring the bells, rouse the town, the players have come.

This was an old saying of mine when I first came with the players to the little township of Kushmire near Bimbel on the Thames, when I was with the Beaumont & Fletcher Company in 1724. Later on I used the phrase again when I brought Sir Henry Irving to Loew's State in Madagascar. And I feel impelled by the same emotion as I welcome you, Sir Laurence, and your fair lady, to this our town. This sweet Hollywood, fairest village of the plain.

As my old friend and pupil, as a matter of fact, Oliver Goldsmith used to say about Auburn.

Yes, many years have gone by and much schnapps has been spilled in dressing rooms since I first went on the stage. I remember when Mr. Burbage first opened the Globe Theatre in London. And I played there for several seasons with Garrick, Kean, and Macready who, in no way, remind me of Benny, Burns and Allen. But there is a tear in my eye when I go to London and stare at the street where stood the old Globe Theatre so proudly, with a little flower shop on one side, the tobacconist on the other, and a little ways up the road, the tavern, where we shouldered the skies and drank our ale.

All this has gone. All this sweet countryside is now an office for Music Corp. of America. But the scent of the old theater stays with me like the scent of the ashes of roses to a lover. And nearby, under the shade of a tree, sheltered from modernity, there is still one old inn that remains untouched and proudly its sign still hangs—The Dragon and The Schmuck. And I used to sit there night after night with Charlie Dickens—anti-Semitic though he was, he loved me. Aye, there we talked. Dickens, Boswell, and Balaban and Katz. Dickens hated Katz more than Balaban.

And in the summertime I used to go to France where the theater was at its peak. The *Comedie Française*, with plays by Molière, Racine, and Dumas—not the kid, but Dumas *père*, the old guy. He was infatuated with Rachel who was appearing in one of his plays. Rachel, the forerunner of all great heroic actresses. Bernhardt and Duse were but pale imitations. I used to kid Dumas a great deal. Bulwer Lytton and myself remembered when he had fallen in love with Betty Hutton.

Ah, yes, those were memories that cannot be taken away from me. This was a happier day, long before the Reds and the goddam television.

But, seriously, may I say to the guest of honor that I have been fortunate in knowing some of the world's greatest men —Messrs. Churchill, Wilson, and Roosevelt—and likewise have I, in my time, seen trod the boards, the world's finest actors—John Barrymore, Gerald du Maurier, and our guest, Laurence Olivier. And somewhere, perhaps not quite so far off stage, the author of your forthcoming play, Theodore Dreiser, will be proud that a creation of his pen takes on full life when you appear in *Sister Carrie.*

America is a rich country, but it is richer indeed now that you, Sir Laurence and Lady Olivier, have again come upon its shores, as will the screen be richer that you both will again be before its cameras. And may the god, Thespis, keep lighting your exits and entrances long after I have gone down the road of my fathers. So be it.

And now, if someone will help me to my carriage, I shall retire—for I am very old and like so, I am very tired.

Good night, my lords and ladies.

17. Lecture at Temple Israel

FRIDAY, JANUARY 4, 1950

SUBJECT: BOOKS BY SHOLEM ASCH

IT IS NO NEW THING that a minstrel or a man who is given to amusement should speak in the synagogue. In years gone by there was always wandering through Middle Europa particularly some mendicant, traveler or peddler, who added to his travail of making a livelihood the art of storytelling—so that after the prayer at sundown *(Maariv)* was said, the storyteller would sit in the corner and by candlelight tell and retell stories old and new that would make the hours pass by happily for his co-religionists who were forced to live by themselves and most of whom seldom ventured to the outside world of the *goyem.*

In the eighteenth century particularly there are many names of these storytellers. Throughout Roumania one Hershel Starpolya was noted for his comic tales. There were many learned men who used synthetic names in their travels and writings—and even in our time, Sholem Aleichem. For while Almighty God in His ways has seen fit to see His earliest followers so long in tears of persecution, He has also invested in them the ability to laugh and has graced them with a sense of humor all through the years—the ability to laugh at their troubles, at their fellow men, and particularly at themselves.

Last week before Master Pierre van Paassen spoke here I was privileged to sit with him at Rabbi Nussbaum's house and as in the days of old, tales were told and I told this one recently sent to me from a friend in Tel Aviv.

Only a short time ago during the battle to save the Holy City, Jews from all lands were forming a barricade and during the lull of the battle many dialects could be distinguished. From the German refugee with his *danka zehr* to the Galitsiana with his own brand of Yiddish. Men, women, and children were fighting this battle and suddenly a woman heavy with child was in labor and a midwife was rushed to her aid and a baby boy was brought into the world. When the dawn came the midwife noticed that the child would not open its right hand and held it tightly clenched. The midwife could do nothing with it and a doctor was sent for who had practiced in Berlin. He looked at the child and then decided perhaps there was some Freudian reason why the child would not open its hand and he questioned the parents (in German). "Where do you come from?" The parents answered, "We are Roumanian Jews from Bucharest."

"Oh," said the doctor, "I'll help the child right away." He stood before the infant, looked at the right hand tightly clenched. He took out his gold watch and held it before the baby. The baby not only opened its hand, but threw out the midwife's earrings.

In Roumania, of course, this story would be told about a Hungarian.

So much for that.

And now to the reason for my occupying this pulpit added to the joy of again celebrating the Sabbath. I had no early religious teaching of any kind. I have had very little schooling of any kind. When I was seven my grandmother, who sleeps now in the lap of God, taught me the morning prayer.

When I was eight I went to school, public school. When I was nine I went on the stage. There was no Bar Mitzvah for me. Nor had I attended one until two years ago. I was not in a temple or a synagogue more than three or four times, until the year 1925, Christian Era, when I appeared in New York in a play called *The Jazz Singer*.

This play was a departure from plays about Jewish people. This was a different story than the ones that had been told on the stage about Hebrews, or as they were once called, *Ibrim*—meaning those from the other side. For this was the story about a boy who gave up all worldly things for the calling of his fathers. Who gave up a great career with great monetary reward as well as cheers from the public to chant in the synagogue to his God. While the play was no great shakes as literature, its emotions were pure and honest. It had a tremendous audience from people of all beliefs, and because of the play's content I found myself called upon to speak in churches as well as temples throughout the country and perforce of that it was necessary for me to know what I was talking about. And so I began to study of the letter of religions in general without much thought at the time of imbibing the spirit. A year or two later I found myself delivering an address at the rabbinical college in Cincinnati. In the last two decades I have acquired I believe one of the largest collections of books on religious subjects—possibly more than anyone in America. And within the last two years I have felt manifested in me the authority to speak up when I find facts completely distorted.

While people can think anything they like, the facts, the written word, which is all men can leave behind them, is open for anyone to read if they want to. There are no secrets or books about Christianity or Judaism or any other religious creed that I know of that cannot be read. Therefore you can know as much as your rabbi or your minister or your priest if you wish to study. You may not feel as deeply or believe as much but you can know what transpired in the past from what men put down in words. So when I read something that may alter or change the thought of my girl-child who is eight, or yours, that I feel is wrong, I do not hesitate to lift both my voice and my pen.

A year and a half ago I challenged the right of the author of *The Big Fisherman* and only lately have I challenged the author of *Mary*. The author of *Mary*, a best seller—and this is to be expected for there has always been a public that will buy a book by a Jew who apologizes for the so-called mistakes of his co-religionists—just like there would no doubt be a big sale in the Deep South for a book by an American Negro who said he was sorry he asked for the right to vote or to be allowed to ride in the streetcar.

In commenting on Sholem Asch and his book *Mary*, I have received many, many letters, most of them in accord with my thinking—a few condemning me, thinking that I have taken umbrage at Mr. Asch because it is said by some that he wishes to become a Christian. This is not so. It is much better to be a good Christian than a misguided Jew. It is much better to be a good anything than to believe wrongly.

I have great sympathy for the *Marranos*, the apostates of the Spanish Inquisition—people who had to give up their religion for another's because the only other alternative was death. I have great respect for those who were brave enough to live, feeling they could do more to earn God's blessing alive than being burned at the stake; and I have alike great feeling for those who had strength enough to believe in the hope of the hereafter. But of all those who became apostates I quote from Heinrich Heine who gave up his faith but whispered to a friend as he did so, "If there was no law against stealing silver I would not have had to do this." And then wrote this. I quote:

"Time was when I had no great love for Moses, no doubt because I was dominated by the Greek spirit and could not forgive the Jewish lawgiver his hatred of images, of the plastic arts. I failed to see that Moses, despite his antagonism to art, was, nevertheless, a great artist himself, endowed with the genuine artistic spirit. With him, as with his Egyptian countrymen, the artistic spirit aimed at the colossal and indestructible. But, unlike the Egyptians, he fashioned his works of art not out of bricks and granite; he built pyramids of humanity, he carved human obelisks, he took a poor race of shepherds and created a nation which would also defy the centuries, a great, eternal, holy nation, a people of God, to serve as an example to all other nations, as a pattern, indeed, to all humanity. He created Israel!

"As of the artist, so also of his creation, the Jews, I have never spoken with sufficient reverence, and again, no doubt, because of my Hellenic temperament, which was repelled by Jewish asceticism. My predilection for Greece has since then waned. I see now that the Greeks were only handsome youths, that the Jews, on the other hand, were always men, strong, inflexible men, not only in those days, but also in the present, in spite of eighteen centuries of persecution and sorrow. I have since learned to appreciate them better; and were it not that champions of revolution and democracy must look upon pride of birth as a foolish contradiction, the writer of these pages might be proud that his forebears belonged to the noble house of Israel, that he is a descendant of the martyrs who gave the world a God and a moral law, who fought and suffered on every battlefield of the spirit." *Heinrich Heine.*

And then there is also the story told in the ghetto of a

time long ago when a missionary was offering twenty dollars for those who would become converted and a Jew who needed medicine money so badly was in line and as the hour grew late he said, "I hope they hurry. I've got to *daven Mincha*" (evening prayer).

Not that the ways and religious customs of our early forefathers were all pure and without the influence of the barbaric age surrounding them. We cannot believe that a just and a kind God could be cajoled into doing a good thing because of people bringing doves or throwing chickens around their head in sacrifice. However, the story of the birth of Christianity is a very simple one and I will not retard the Sabbath prayer by attempting a series of parables but only to briefly repeat what most of you know or could learn.

Under the heel of the Roman Empire the peoples of Judea were hoping and praying for some heroic figure to lead them into freedom. Someone from the line of King David, the illustrious David whose career as soldier, poet, and psalmist has never been surpassed even though his personal life might be challenged at least from the standpoint of the moral code of our day. However, there is no question that among the many young men who gave of their hearts' blood there must have been someone like this simple carpenter Yoshe, much later called Jesus who, having lived a most ascetic life, hoped to save his people because of his earnestness and unswerving belief in Jewry. (It is written of Him that He said, "I have come to fulfill the law, not to destroy it.") But because the people wanted a military leader, they said, "He is from the line of David. He will fight for us. He will be our King"—then the Roman government did away with this sweet young man and put on his cross "King of the Jews." And since the Roman government was in the habit and since it was the custom to do away with political prisoners in this manner it caused no great stir in the communities. Therefore it has not been found in the records anywhere. Even though the Jewish historian Josephus saw fit or someone else did to interpolate into his writings some few words as to Him.

However, Christianity blazed into the world when about thirty or forty years later, Saulus (called Saul), later called Paulus (Paul), a Jew of Greek citizenry, when traveling on the road between Taursus and Damascus was felled to the ground and saw before him a strange light and a vision in which the Rabbi Jesus spoke to him and admonished him for persecuting his followers.

(It is George Moore's theory in the book *The Brook Kerith* that Saul did not see the vision, but actually met Jesus on the road—for Moore believes that he did not die upon the Cross, but was taken by Joseph of Arimathaea, and Nicodemus, and was healed of his wounds; and went to live with a cult called the Essenes, who were a tribe of Jews who lived an ascetic existence.)

Saul was completely converted, but found favor mostly in his own country, Greece, where his followers were first Jews and then Gentiles. From then on the Hellenistic Greeks took over and the simple Carpenter whose name must have been Joshua—Joseph—Yoshe, became Jesus, and the Apostles and the followers were all given names according to the Greek. They were all pious Orthodox Jews with Hebrew or Aramaic names, with the possible exception of Matti, who was later known as Matthew. Some scholars say, however, that he was also a devout Jew and a Levite. From then on, most of these simple teachings of the young Rabbi were embellished and embellished.

The Greeks added many things, and the pagans who became converted believed many more. There have been many crucified Gods—fifteen or sixteen—long before Christianity, and there are millions who believe they were all born immaculately and all resurrected. Pictures and paintings have been created of these disciples and their Saviour that could bear no possible resemblance to those simple Jews from Nazareth, Galilee or the nearby cities. And then all sorts of sayings, proverbs, admonitions, and sermons were accredited to this group and the simple carpenter, most of which the great teacher Hillel had said more than a hundred years before. But that is not important. If your table is prepared well what difference does it make who the cook was? If we suddenly discovered Puccini did not compose "Mme. Butterfly" it wouldn't make it one note less melodic. And so if my daughter would believe and would live according to the Scriptures, actually it is not important for her to be sure of who said what or when—but she must not be told that her father's forefathers were unbelievers, infidels, and are now very sorry about it.

The reason why I feel impelled to speak of *The Big Fisherman* and of Sholem Asch's *Mary*, I repeat, is because of my child and yours, particularly mine whose mother is non-Jewish. If this child will read two books by two great Christian clergymen—Pierre Van Paassen's book *Why Jesus Died* and Dr. Harry Emerson Fosdick's *The Man from Nazareth* —she can follow what is written in these books and become a good Christian and a good Jewess and a good woman. But if she reads the books I shall speak about tonight she must perforce come away with other opinions, particularly after reading Sholem Asch. Her opinions would be that the forefathers of her father, mine, were misguided, wrong, and in a measure that's why they've been persecuted through the years. That the great culture that the sages of the

Hebrews have given to the world is completely unimportant in comparison to what the new group created in the first century A.D. and again in the 17th century. If she accepts what is written emotionally she might even become anti-Semitic.

Let us take *The Big Fisherman.* Poor Simon, strong, gaunt fisherman—Jewish to the core—hoping only for the Messiah to come and free Israel of its bondage, suddenly becomes on paper Petros, he of the Rock, Peter—and in Mr. Douglas' book we find him in Rome speaking Greek, Latin—a great martyr for something that there are no records of any kind to show he knew anything about, or could have known anything about. So this was my letter published in the New York *Times* in 1948 . . .

"About twenty-three years ago I appeared as an actor in a play by Samson Raphaelson called *The Jazz Singer.* Because this play was about a boy who came from generations of religious singers of the synagogue, I began to take an interest in religious books and acquired a large library of Christianity and Judaism. Again and again I read books about Jesus by Renan, Moore, Klausner—these three particularly because one feels so much compassion for Jesus due to their sympathetic and warm pens. Books with the Papini kind of writing leave one cold, for they take this simple, lovable, Godlike, humble Jewish carpenter and make him seem like a white-robed Houdini. Therefore I could not wait to read *The Big Fisherman* and it has given me a great deal to think over.

"First, because this Simon (whom the Greeks many, many years later called Peter) is not in any way the Simon that I had read and thought about in the past, and because of the book *The Big Fisherman* being such a great success, my taking it to task will not have any effect at all. And being a commercial showman in every respect, as a publisher I wish I were publishing the book. As the owner of a book shop, I'd like to have my shelves full of it. But as to having written it, this is something else again. For while I believe that the theater and so many of the arts should at all times be commercial, a book about Simon, later to be called Peter and sainted—yes, this is something else again.

"The Simon I had pictured—and surely he must be pictured so—was a tall, gaunt, simple Hebrew fisherman who, like most of his neighbors, was suffering under the yoke of Roman oppression, and being a most religious and zealous Jew, he too believed that a Messiah had to come to fulfill the promises of the old prophets. And this Simon gave up his trade and everything else to follow the young rabbi, Jesus. And humbly and simply they sat at the Passover, all orthodox, religious Jews. I cannot for one moment picture this Simon (so much later to be called Peter by the Greeks) to be the one that Mr. Douglas has written about. I have a feeling that this book should have been written near the River Jordan or perhaps in the ghetto near the East River of New York. I felt so often in reading *The Big Fisherman* that it was written close to the tracks of the Boston & Maine Railroad during the cold winter.

"Some years ago I read in German, Shakespeare's *The Merchant of Venice* and there was a foreword by Heinrich Heine in which he wrote:

"'After seeing *The Merchant of Venice* I walked along the Rialto looking to find a Shylock lamenting upon the loss of his ducats and instead I found him in the synagogue wailing, bemoaning only the loss of his daughter Jessica.' These few words of Heine's came to me as I was thinking about Simon (so much later to be called Peter by the Greeks) and I thought to myself if the good Lord spares me until

my daughter is happily married, I shall go and spend the
rest of my days in the Holy Land and wander from town
to town hoping to find the likeness of Simon, but I have a
feeling that if I do he will be more like this description of
a ferryman Sholem Asch wrote about long ago in *Tales of
My People*.

"In the summer he earns his living from the river. All week
long he is in his little boat with the sail that cuts the sky
in two. On the Sabbath, the river behaves like a good Jew.
The river observes the Sabbath and the holy days. She is
quiet. One wave gently kisses the other, and the ferryman
and his wife sit by their door. He recites the Sabbath prayer,
and his wife reads from the women's portion, and they
speak of God's wonders to the waves. And each wave picks
up a word and says amen."

"GEORGE JESSEL"

And my reason for writing this and for taking this tone
is mostly for the sake of my daughter whose mind is in a
plastic stage. I want her to know that this Simon called
Peter was a good man and a religious man and believed in
the God of Israel . . . and not that he condemned most of
his fellow Jews, discarded the Jewish religion, and for that
was made the Keeper of the Keys of Heaven.

And now comes a book by a formerly warm, gifted Rus-
sian-Polish orthodox Jew—Sholem Asch, with whom thinking
people must disagree. And I don't think I need say anything else but give you my comment on it which was printed
in the New York *Times*:

"Having had the privilege of making myself heard through
your weekly Book Review in the past, I take advantage of
another opportunity to offer you my comments, this time
on the book *Mary* by Sholem Asch.

"Strange things happen to men of letters as they approach age. Some, like Mr. Shaw, cuddle closer to fundamentals and facts, some become completely bewildered, and some suddenly search for spiritual salvation. The latter, I think, is what has happened to Sholem Asch whose early works as a storyteller and novelist were so promising and about whom in an interview I said:

" 'The Yiddish jargon takes on great beauty from the pen of Sholem Asch. The reader feels the warm patois of the ghetto come through in the translation, as if Theodore Dreiser were writing in Yiddish.'

"In the past few years Mr. Asch's complete change of style and mood have made me wonder, particularly after reading his latest, *Mary*. I think Mr. Asch has been hypnotized by the Hellenistic Greek writers of the accepted first century. Either that, or perhaps like the Greek Jew Saul on the road to Damascus, scenes from beyond this vale were revealed to him. If so, this would give him the right to write as he does in the style of Luke and Mark and Matthew, all of whom were anything but eyewitnesses. Personally I cannot be reconciled that Mr. Asch believes the words he puts into the mouths of Mary and the simple Galileans. It does not seem possible that the author who knew so well the Jews of the Warsaw ghetto and of Eastern Europe could make the peasants of Nazareth and Bethlehem and Jerusalem speak as though they had read the New Testament.

"Perhaps Mr. Asch has found the religion of his childhood not tangible enough for his needs. If so, I believe it would help him to read *The Pharisees* by the great Rabbi Leo Baeck, who does so much for those who want to believe in the New Testament when he says: 'What had begun with imagination had been completed by faith.' Were I not contemporary with Mr. Asch and did I not know that he was the writer of a great book called *Mottke Gonif* and other great folk tales which endeared him to me, I would say after finishing *Mary* that this book was written by order of a Spanish Inquisitor in the fifteenth century who stood behind Reb Asch and guided his quill."

"Sincerely and respectfully,
"GEORGE JESSEL"

Oh, someday I would like to take Mr. Asch with me to the Conservatory of Art in Cleveland and show him a work of sculpture by Max Kalish in which the Rabbi Jesus steps down from the cross and points accusingly. The figure is called *The Militant Christ*, the inscription reads, "What have ye done in my name?"

So be it. I am very privileged indeed to have been given this opportunity of speaking in this untarnished house. And may the Lord continue to shine His countenance on this congregation and its fine rabbi and his wife and daughter, and his splendid *Kaddish*.

It has been handed down to us by the sages of old, the cardinal benediction that in all times praise the Lord. In times of great joy and sorrow alike. At the birth of the newborn—at the passing of the old. This evening has been one of joy to me that I have been given the privilege to speak with my heart and my mind.

Therefore—(in Hebrew) "Hear, oh Israel, the Lord our God, the Lord is One . . . Amen."

With Lois and Jerilynn.

A visit to Israel with Jerilynn who was then 10 years old.

With June Haver during the shooting of *I Wonder Who's Kissing Her Now.*

With Darryl F. Zanuck at the Man-of-the-Year Dinner in Hollywood.

With Ezio Pinza at the opening of *Tonight We Sing*.

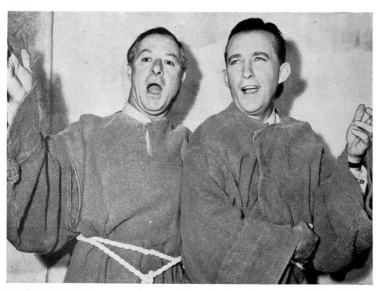

With Bing Crosby at the time of the founding of the
Friars' Club in Hollywood.

With Cardinal McIntyre of California at a hospital benefit dinner.

With Moshe Sharett in Tel-Aviv in 1953.

With Rocky Marciano.

Awarding plaque to Joe DiMaggio the night of his last appearance in Yankee uniform.

With James J. Walker, then Mayor of New York, at the Stork Club.

Campaigning with President Truman in 1948.

With Marilyn Monroe at her first big Hollywood party at the
Beverly Wilshire Hotel.

Last appearance with Al Jolson at the Oriental Theater, Chicago, 1950.

With George M. Cohan and friends at Jessel's Bowery Café, New York World's Fair, 1939.

Friars' Dinner to George Jessel at the Waldorf-Astoria in 1954 with Helen Hayes, Fred Allen, Jack Benny, Eddie Fisher, Bob Hope, Ted Lewis, Danny Kaye, and Jessie Block.

18. Friars' Club Dinner for George Jessel. Waldorf-Astoria

FEBRUARY 21, 1954

THIS DINNER WAS GIVEN by the Friars of New York with proceeds to the Heart Fund. Speakers included Jack Benny, Bob Hope, Fred Allen, Danny Kaye, Mayor Robert Wagner, Oscar Hammerstein the II, Robert Weitman, Tony Martin, Eddie Fisher, Ted Lewis, Senator Warren Magnuson, and Miss Helen Hayes.

The following is Jessel's speech, after accepting the Humanitarian Award:

Mr. Toastmaster, distinguished and learned public servants, captains of industry, the first lady of the theater, fellow players and you, madames and messieurs, who have definitely manifested your affection for me . . . you paid to come in . . . with the currency of the realm, I have been sitting here with the patience of a Mrs. Judge Crater, listening to a mass of oratory in its adolescence, and being ofttimes in a mood religious, the words of the prophet Jeremiah in their original tongue kept passing through my mind, "Oh, how long, O Lord?" and from on high came the answer to him, "*Shma, chi-vechayem*"—"Live, listen, and endure."

I have been piqued by hearing so often, "It's about time they gave him a dinner." This is the thirty-third dinner in the last six years in which cold food and warm words have been hurled in my direction. Ofttimes I have been made guest of honor at the eleventh hour when the real guy didn't show up and they marched me in with the dessert. No man has felt like a Jewish Baked Alaska as often as I have. And many times I felt it was my own head on the tray, instead of the Cherries Jubilee or the leaking ice donkey. Therefore, I am not quite in the emotional state of most men under these circumstances, who don't know what to say at a time like this. I have words, not only for this affair, but also for a speech at the Starlight Roof, where I am going as soon as I leave here.

My career has found me as quick to respond to an introduction as a soldier to a military command. My friends, throughout my life I have found myself constantly mounted for a verbal encounter. I don't believe there is a person on this dais that I have not functioned for as a herald to have them speak at an occasion in their honor. I believe that nearly all of these seated here have had dinners for them, with the exception of Fred Allen, and this is only because the Knights of Columbus are not quite as active as the Jewish Theatrical Guild.

I have made speeches in many parts of the world and often for monetary compensation, and perforce of this motley reward, I have had to hurl adjectives and shout praises of the virtues of men in whose hearts these virtues were nonexistent, and ofttimes had to hide their vices under my own conscience. In the last three years I have spoken more than six hundred times and mostly on one subject—aid to the democracy of Israel. In seventy cities in sixty-eight days I raised over thirty million dollars. This money came only from people of my own religious persuasion. I believe I have tugged at both the hearts and the pockets of every Jew that can afford to give. I left no Cohen unturned. This has not been an easy task, because at every place where I have spoken, with the exception of a temple or synagogue, there was a dinner or a luncheon, and going through these daily is a baptismal fire that I wouldn't even wish upon the people who make up the television ratings.

Firstly, there is the well-meaning group who have prepared the affair long in advance and they want it to be an evening to be remembered and a memory to conjure with. Incidentally, I have found this phrase to fit into every speech I have ever made.

But, back to the meetings. So there is a meeting before the luncheon or dinner begins, where the agenda is decided. Just a few people will say a few words, I am told, or maybe just bow. Then I will be presented to deliver my message so I can journey on to the next hamlet. But, this doesn't go like this. Oh, no, first the chairlady gets up and welcomes everybody and then starts to thank her coworkers for what they have contributed to make the affair such a great success, which it hasn't been, because it didn't start yet. She thanks everyone in the building and an aunt and uncle from out of town, and then presents one of the local rabbis to speak the invocation and bless the bread.

Now the choosing of the particular member of the clergy has not been easy, because of what particular denomination he is and as to how many of the big *machers* go to his particular temple. Anyway, that's over. He speaks, and with all due fairness and in complete tolerance, may I say that these gentlemen are to be forgiven if added to the blessing of the bread they venture some part of a forthcoming sermon.

And this sermon is often interspersed with the first act of *King Lear* and the last two acts of *The Ice Man Cometh*. But this, too, is to be forgiven, because one must realize that in the average city the local rabbi so seldom has as big an audience as would gather to hear a minstrel of any consequence passing through but for the hour. Only on the Holy Day of Atonement does he find such an audience and that only at the mass for the departed.

And then again, there are the kindly forewarnings that I receive before my speech, "Mr. Jessel, we don't want to tell you, of course, how or what to say, but this is a peculiar town, hardly any of us understand any jargon. We're sort of different. You see, this temple is so-and-so, this synagogue is so-and-so." And in one little town I found a group of my coreligionists so reformed that they had a sign in front of the temple "Closed during the Jewish holidays." But, nevertheless, the speeches have been all to the good, and the end more than justifies the means.

And so, I would be most remiss emotionally if I didn't honestly admit to you that behind this seemingly self-assured manner of mine, and behind this seeming attitude of complete relaxation, there is both a tingling of the nerves and a completely thankful heart that you have come here tonight, that you have come in my name to a dinner in which there will be a large bounty for those less fortunate. For, though there are many dinners in many men's honor, these men, like myself, have some small virtue. I cannot remember anyone ever giving a dinner for Jack, the Ripper.

And I am most proud of the character and caliber of those of you in the hall and particularly am I complimented by the distinguished group that are closer to me. Of course, there are a lot of other people that were supposed to come, but couldn't because of political commitments miles away on the morrow. So there are always last-minute surprises at these dinners. Instead of people you invited, other people come. I expected Mr. Truman and Mr. Stevenson, and I got

Tony Martin and Eddie Fisher. Had I invited Sir Winston Churchill, Myron Cohen would have come in his place.

But, most seriously and in complete honesty, these things do a great deal of good, because they bring men and women together with no malice aforethought; and while there are many who decry this age with its mad pace and its atomic energy, the world has improved and man's kinship to man is today made of sterner stuff than it was even ten years ago. In many cases men have become even kinder to all things that are mortal as in comparison to the old days, when life of any kind had such little value. Only a few men had feeling for all things that live and gave them value, and deservedly so, because they were created by God. These men stand out, almost alone in the passing of one hundred years: Robert Burns, who wrote an ode to a mouse. The poem encompasses this verse:

> I'm truly sorry man's dominion
> Has broken Nature's social union,
> An' justifies that ill opinion,
> Which makes thee startle
> At me, thy poor, earth-born companion,
> An' fellow-mortal.

And William Blake:

> Tiger! Tiger! burning bright,
> In the forests of the night, . . .
> Did He who made the Lamb, make thee?

And this also from Blake:

> Little fly, thy summer's play
> My thoughtless hand has brushed away.

I give you my solemn word, my lords and ladies, I would rather have been a contemporary or even the printer's devil to Robert Burns and William Blake than to have the combined Flindex, Nielsen, and Hooper ratings of Gleason, Space Patrol, Dragnet, Pinky Lee, and Howdy Doody.

And so, I would bare my soul to you, for there will be no more such occasions at which the spotlight shall be turned full upon me. This is the third dinner that the Friars have given me in my more than forty-five years in the amusement business. The first was in 1927 and the people who sat close to me were very close to my heart, and I am lonely for them tonight. I miss them so much: Jimmy Walker, Sam Harris, William Morris, Sime Silverman, Ben Bernie, Gus Edwards, and last, but surely not least, the noblest Friar of them all, George M. Cohan.

But the balance is on the joy side, for with all the scars that sometimes incidents burn into the heart and soul of a man, the last dozen years have been exceptionally kind, and I am humbly grateful. While I am not a rich man, I show a profit. I had nothing like this when I was born. And my thinking has gone to a much higher plane than it was years ago. I am much more concerned with tomorrow's prayers than with yesterday's roses. I am most content with both the present and the future, that I have been blessed with a daughter who in her dozen years here shows every sign of being my comfort in the twilight of my life.

I want to thank those who spoke. The speeches were good and most deserving. I am happy that so many of the speakers are not from the theatrical world alone, as I would like to feel that whatever I have contributed has been spread on a broader canvas and hasn't been limited to the proscenium arch. So many of us live our entire lives, on and off, within the four walls of the theater. A vaudeville actor, I understand, entered a hotel room, picked up the Gideon Book, and told his partner it was by Abel Green and Joe Laurie, Jr.—"Bible Biz."

No, I have but few virtues. I was a good son, I hope I am a good father, and I am an expert in the art of timing. And thus do I take my leave of the speaker's pulpit with a new thought that has just come to me—this is an evening to be remembered and a memory to conjure with.

You will remember, Jeri dear, that our TV director, Manny Manheim, told you to be sure and bow when the applause came at the end of our show. You felt sort of awkward about this, but you won't if you continue to be in the amusement business. . . . And the longer you stay in it, the more you will want to take bows. Actors and actresses never get too old to tell about them, and the curtain calls they have taken, and often add on a few without any qualms, like the beginner at golf who knocks off three or four strokes on his score card on every hole.

And so, as an interested audience for all the amusement arts, I present to you the following.

19. Curtain Calls

IN THE GENERAL CONVERSATION of people who are interested in the theater, the inevitable subject is: "Where's the talent coming from?"

There are no more minor leagues where talent can be developed. There isn't one vaudeville theater left in the U.S.A. The idea of a Danny Kaye or a Judy Garland bringing vaudeville back in the Palace in New York is about as absurd an expression as I've ever heard. These great artists simply give a recital or concert and, as a curtain-raiser, have four acts or so, and then they come on for the rest of the evening. If this is vaudeville, my Uncle Max is Rubirosa.

There are no more burlesque theaters which, in former years, brewed the potion that poured itself into the theater with the thunder of Niagara Falls—from the days of David Warfield, Sam Bernard, the four Cohans, and, in my time, Fannie Brice, Sophie Tucker, Clark and McCullough, James Barton, Bert Lahr, Jack Pearl, and scores of others.

There is no longer a third, or fourth company of musical successes, wherein there would be discovered stars of the future. There are no longer Chicago productions; in the old days thirty or forty musical plays would be produced and would come out of Chicago. This was a most fertile soil for stars in the making. There are even very few musical plays produced any longer in New York, for the simple reason that the cost of the gamble is much too great. Even the legitimate plays, with one stage set, have to be sponsored by some thirty or forty backers. The average one-set play today costs between seventy-five and one hundred thousand dollars to bring into New York, after a week or two on the road, whereas my first legitimate play, *The Jazz Singer*, presented by Sam Harris, Lewis and Gordon and staged by Albert Lewis, played three weeks out of town and opened at the Fulton Theatre in New York at a cost of less than ten thousands dollars. *Turn to the Right*, a bigger success, cost even less.

The stock company—and there was one in at least one hundred cities in America—is also a thing of the past, and I think that if, someday, people will start to excavate parking lots, I am sure they will find the remnants of a stock theater underneath.

During the past two years I spoke in more than one hundred cities, on a tour for "Aid to Israel," and in every town, I asked what had happened to such and such a theater I used to play in; and the answer invariably was, "It is a parking lot now . . ."

The only two theatrical reservoirs that show promise

are the summer theaters and the borsch circuit, although the summer theater too, is mostly dependent on the star system, using names rather than new faces. The borsch circuit, which consists of some summer hotels in the Catskill Mountains where they have week-end performances, has brought forth a lot of ambitious kids, but all of them are almost identically cut from the same pattern and completely lacking in gentility. Of all of them, Buddy Hackett has a chance. He is a pudgy, cute young fellow from Brooklyn and looks kind of like a happy Chinese Jew; and if given an opportunity to play before audiences other than those who frequent the Catskills, he could be something.

So, the fact that some real theatrical talent has emerged in America in the last dozen years is amazing, for first of all, the actor or actress has no place to get experience, and if one out of ten thousand does get a break in a Broadway success, within the first three days there comes an offer from a picture company or a television show of such financial size that it cannot be turned down—because it certainly would not be fair to the actor's or the actress' relatives.

The radio has brought little if anything to the art of acting. You cannot learn to live a character, and play it sincerely, with a microphone half an inch from your mouth. TV so far has developed nothing, with the possible exception of Jack Webb, who gives a fine performance of a modern young cop but may never have to learn to say anything else but, "I'm Friday, I'll be back Tuesday."

And then again, as I have previously stated (and will no doubt state again), the art of acting for TV is always based on an eighth point up or an eighth point down on the surveys and on the idiosyncrasies of sponsorships.

And as for really natural singing voices, the first thing you are taught on the radio is to keep it down, and if necessary the control room will build it up. For example, many years ago, B.M. (Before the Microphone), I was at the Ritz-Carlton in Atlantic City, watching a floor show in which the inimitable Joe Frisco was appearing. I was sitting with Irving Berlin, and Frisco introduced Mr. Berlin, who arose and said he would sing his latest composition—whereupon Frisco quipped, "You will have to come and hug him if you want to hear him . . ." When I heard Mr. Berlin last year on the radio, his voice was "goosed up" so that many people thought it was Mario Lanza.

Eddie Fisher, who has refused to croon and nearly always sings in full voice, has made a big hit and may continue to do so if they don't tire him out too soon. Only lately he appeared on two TV shows—one in New York, one in California—gave a recital at the Hollywood Bowl, played three benefits, made a half-dozen recordings, all in one week. They make him do so many things in so little time, you would think Hitler and his gang were around the corner.

Yet, with all this, there have been a few amazingly talented people come through the last dozen years.

The biggest dramatic talent, as actor-director and writer as well, who has not earned the success his versatility deserves, is Orson Welles. Because of his many facets, he never gave any one of them enough chance to pour forth gold—even though it must have been great fun for him, while playing Othello at night, to give a magic show in the morning and teach fencing in the afternoon. Loving him as much as I do, I would rather settle for Othello or even Lear.

Welles spends most of his time in Italy and France now. Some wag in Rome told me only a few months ago, when I inquired of Orson: "Mr. Welles has gone back to Paris, to the Père Lachaise cemetery, to dig up Alexandre Dumas' mustache . . ." I hope someday Orson will come back to the

American Theatre, or I will even settle to see him on TV, provided the manuscripts and the production are in his own hands, and not rewritten to suit Mrs. Klinck, who is the wife of Mr. Klinck, the owner of Klinck's Disappearing Undershirts. For Welles still could have greatness in his own country and could be a sober John Barrymore or a kindly Richard Mansfield. I hope he will return very soon and give his countrymen a little more chance to meet him, artistically, halfway.

Now, after Mr. Welles and his self-imposed exile to Loew's Elba and Pantages' Capri, there is Jose Ferrer, who is the best technical actor and most versatile that has been around in a long, long time. Not since George M. Cohan has there been such a versatile fellow as Jose—and while he never quite breaks your heart in anything, he at all times holds your interest and makes you profoundly respect him, whether it be as a Hungarian composer in a motion picture or as Cyrano de Bergerac on the stage.

For the next duo I choose David Wayne and Marlon Brando.

Wayne, like Ferrer, is also a most versatile actor. While not as technically facile as Ferrer, he makes it up by having a great deal of heart. Three of his performances stand out way up high—his playing of the little fellow in *Finian's Rainbow,* a musical fantasy, was a delight. In the motion picture, *Wait 'til the Sun Shines, Nellie,* he showed an emotional depth, and his interpretation of the little Illinois barber was so true that I have heard a whole audience weep louder than the popping of the popcorn. I saw this picture with audiences more than half a dozen times, and Wayne never failed to break my heart. (It also broke my heart that I produced the picture, for it was not a financial success!) And, finally, his performance in *Teahouse of the*

August Moon on Broadway, which won him the kudos of the public and of the critics.

Brando is something else again. I saw him in *A Streetcar Named Desire*, and he was Brando, playing an illiterate, and he was great—but he was Brando. I saw him in the picture *Julius Caesar*, and he was great—but he was Brando. I saw him in the picture *Waterfront*, and he was the same Brando —but always compelling, always fascinating. So was George Arliss the same person in *Disraeli, Rothschild, The Devil, The Green Goddess, Alexander Hamilton*—and he was wonderful, too.

On the romantic side, no handsome leading man after the manner of Otis Skinner, Henry Miller, William Faversham, or Edgar Selwyn of the old days has appeared on the horizon —not even has there been any up-and-coming leading men appearing on the stage with the carriage of a Freddie March, or the Clark Gable who played in *Machinal*. There is just nobody around but one—and this is Alfred Drake, who recently was in a musicalization of the Otis Skinner success *Kismet*, the only one around since Dennis King who can enter with a swirling cape and a low bow, and is an actor of infinite charm, with a lovely singing voice. I would like to see him someday play Cyrano and if I could dig up the money, I would present him in a revival of *Robin Hood*— and I *may*.

In the lighter field, there has emerged the greatest lyric entertainer of his time—a young man most attractive to look upon, who runs completely the gamut in the entertainment field. He can speak to an audience with the dignity of a cardinal and, in the snap of a finger, sing *Minnie the Moocher* with the abandon of a Louis Armstrong. He has never uttered a line or ventured a gesture that would embarrass the most sensitive. He is not only the greatest entertainer of this, our time, but of all the men who have ever appeared alone on the stage to entertain an audience, only Al Jolson had a greater gift than Danny Kaye—for Jolson was more emotional and physical as against Kaye's dignity and personal charm.

And now we come to Dean Martin and Jerry Lewis. There is no question about the potential of these two young men. I don't believe that Lewis' talents have been fully tapped, and it is quite possible that they never will be. These fellows are in motion pictures, night clubs, TV, making zillions of dollars, so that I doubt whether there will be an urge to develop or polish any further.

In the Cohan style, charming song-and-dance man with a serious note behind him, there is Dan Dailey and Donald O'Connor. Dailey, successful on the screen, and O'Connor both on the screen and on TV—both very earnest about their business, and they will, I believe, reach greater heights and larger audiences as they go on.

Among the ladies, there aren't many to write about in the last dozen years. There is no new Judy Garland, no Ethel Merman, and certainly no Helen Hayes or Katharine Cornell.

The young English actress, Audrey Hepburn, is full of theater greatness, but she is an English actress.

Renée Jeanmaire, on the lighter side, is also from Europe, and so is Deborah Kerr, who has everything, but they are all from over the sea, where people still pay more attention to the English Channel than to channel 2-4-7 like most of us at home.

So, these lovely ladies cannot be included in the American scene.

Julie Harris shows promise as a stage actress.

Grace Kelly has achieved stardom in what seems like to be an hour and a half. The ad in the trade paper, *Variety*, put in by Paramount Studios, has her appearing in three or four pictures, one after the other. While I would love to see her in a play, I doubt whether this will ever come to pass.

Abigail "Tommye" Adams, who, if she had the urge or had started off with the breaks in her favor, showed every promise of being a fine screen actress, which would have surely prompted an ambition in her to go into the theater.

And in the next dozen years, if she keeps her poise and continues to be as articulate as she has been on her few performances on TV, I think Jerilynn Jessel has a chance to be something, since she shows every promise that she will look like her mother and be as shy as I am—and it's a good thing that this is not the other way around . . .

And now we come to the most important factor: the men who create, who put the words on paper—for without them, there is nothing.

The last dozen years have much to be saluted for in Tennessee Williams, whose great imaginative and sensitive pen has given to us three great plays, showing tremendous feeling and the power to drill deep in the wells of human emotion: *The Glass Menagerie, A Streetcar Named Desire, Rose Tattoo,* all amazing pieces of theatrical writing. It was my privilege to be the speaker at a dinner given in Mr. Williams' honor, and I wish I had almost gone overboard in my speech about his art as I am doing now. But it was a very gay evening that called for brevity as far as speaking was concerned. But I did make him laugh with the following: "Mr. Tennessee Williams and I have a good deal in common. I am also a writer and come from a family of writers—particularly my Uncle Ohio Levine, who after seeing *A Streetcar Named Desire* is writing a play entitled *A Steam Engine Called Sam.*"

The next young man with great feeling for drama, though less spectacular, is Arthur Miller, whose *Death of a Salesman* had much of the same strength and honest quality as Mr. Williams' plays.

Robert Anderson showed great promise in *Tea and Sympathy*, then came up with a dull one; but I feel sure he will score again.

On the lighter side, there is the comedian-song writer-stage director-librettist, and Broadwayite, Abe Burrows, whose collaboration on *Guys and Dolls* and other work in the theater promise things to come that will be even more important.

Of the song writers and composers, Frank Loesser is the only one around who seems to be able to be both lyricist and composer, with the energy of Cohan, Berlin, and Cole Porter. He has not touched your heart with his songs as yet, but I am sure he will as time goes by.

Messers. Adler and Ross, who have written the music and lyrics for *The Pajama Game* are names and talents to be watched.

As for theatrical producers, the last dozen years have produced no Sam Harris, no Arthur Hopkins, no Jed Harris, no Max Gordon, nobody whom I can think of. And the only posy I can throw is to Martin and Feuer, who showed great energy and a love for the theater with *Guys and Dolls*, *Can-Can*, three new productions in the making, and the importation from London of a play called *The Girl Friend*. This is quite a gamble, and there will have to be a great deal of work to make it worth seven dollars and seventy cents in New York. It has a chance only if the opening night audience loves satire, and if the *Times* and the *Tribune* rave—and even then it might find itself after a time with a limited audience, as was the case with *The Skin of Your Teeth*. (I may have to eat these words, but there may not be anything else to eat, so it won't be so bad.) *

* Author's Note: P.S. Much time has elapsed. I am eating the words.

As far as stage directors are concerned, there is only one that I can see who rates with Arthur Hopkins, Jed Harris, George S. Kaufman, Albert Lewis, or any of the fellows who were staging plays fifteen to twenty years ago: Elia Kazan, who not only is the greatest stage director of his time but has done the most important trick of being able to direct great motion pictures as well. So few have been able to do both. The confines of the four walls of the theater and the great canvas of the screen have been no problem to Kazan. This little guy is definitely to the theater born, and does things with a realism that would have made Belasco turn his collar around.

As for dramatic criticism, no new critic of any consequence has caused any furor. The theater being smaller all the time, there is evidently no desire for anyone to become a dramatic critic. And what a pity! There is now no George Jean Nathan, Ashton Stevens, Alec Woollcott, Percy Hammond, or even an Amy Leslie in the offing. There are a zillion columnists—three or four in almost every town—and that is where their column will stay. There is no Arthur Brisbane or O. O. McIntyre around or even in the making.

As for hangouts on Broadway, the last dozen years have only brought out Toots Shor, on 51st Street. Mr. Shor's complete disregard for his amount of praising and insulting has made his diner the popular hangout for the sports world, the newspaper gang, and men like myself, who will drink with anyone, salute anything that happened in the past, and cry at the slightest rumor that a stranger in Yucatan may be dying.

In Hollywood, there is Jack's at the Beach and the *Luau*, where they serve a drink called "Gold Cup" and if you drink three, you better get mail in the morning or you won't know who you are.

Young lady, just a few days ago, when I visited you and your mother and her handsome young husband, Major Leonard Kleckner, you were all excited about going to a dance, and you told me about some boy who is not nearly as good-looking as the Alexander kid from Hollywood. No, he was not as strong-looking, nor did he have those soft eyes, but he was awfully cute.

And so, may I tell you something about some ladies that I have looked forward to meeting—some of them cute, and some of them strong-looking, with eyes like the Alexander kid.

I heard you once say to your mother, "Daddy flirted with everybody!" Well, many actors do that, and it does not do much harm. And sometimes a little flirtation that never goes any further leaves such a pleasant memory. For example, here are a few lines from a speech made by the First Lady of the stage, Miss Helen Hayes, at the Friars' Heart Fund dinner, given to me not so long ago:

"I feel that I should be very dignified and very impressive—that seems to me the only excuse for my jumping to my feet and interrupting this great flow of wit. I should be paying a very elegant tribute to Georgie and his unique contribution to the theater and to the merriment of this country that he loves, etc. But I'm not going to—because there's another tribute that I want to pay Georgie that's a little nearer to my heart. And I never thought of it until last week when we met on the street, quite by chance, and we were talking about this dinner, and I told him that I was a little self-conscious about being up on the dais and being so prominent in this way, because I wasn't able to get to Jack Benny's dinner last year, as much as I wanted, and here I was going to be on Jack's television show next week, and, well, I was just really very embarrassed about it.

"And Georgie said, 'Never mind Benny. I've known

you longer than he has—and anyway, I was in love with you once in Cleveland.'

"So there we stood on 52nd Street, looking down over the years, and I remembered a week in Cleveland that was, well, it was kind of prismatic in its sparkle and color and joyousness—and the laughs, oh, the laughs! We had both been playing there in our respective plays. I hasten to add that we hadn't spent one minute alone together. But at the end of that week I went away from Cleveland quite happily bemused. So I turned to Jessel on 52nd Street, and said, 'Well, you know something, Georgie. I was in love with you in Cleveland.'

"Georgie thought a minute and then he said, 'I wonder what would have happened if we'd been booked into Erie.'

"But I'm here tonight to say that I'm grateful to a kind destiny that allowed me the opportunity to be in love with Georgie for one week in my life. I think that every young woman some time in her growing up should be in love with Georgie Jessel for one week— one week. . . ."

20. A Dozen Roses—Maybe More

"An Ode to a Girdle"

That which her slender waist confined
does now my wishful thinking bind—
A little band that nestles where
all that's good and all that's fair.
Would that I had what this ribband bound
take all the rest as the sun goes 'round.

(with apologies to Edmund Waller—
17th Century)

SOME PEOPLE IN THE amusement business eternally stick their chins out so that they may be poked at in the press—and even when they don't, most newspapers, even in sweet Hollywood, find some way to link something rotten to show business in general.

Any woman found frozen to death in the alley was either a former Ziegfeld Girl, a starlet, or a stand-in for a star, so that the headlines may read: "NORMA PICKFORD'S . . ." then, in very small letters, " . . . former stand-in, found in sewer."

In my case most of the columnists seemed to have found me useful as a companion of some lovely damsels. I don't complain about this, but in ninety-nine out of a hundred cases, while the fine young lady might have been out on the town with some other chap, I was either working on a speech, watching a ball game, or playing gin at the Hillcrest Country Club. But it would be ungallant for me ever to make denials, and when I have done so, it has not been publicly, but over the phone to some jealous gentleman who is saying: "What were you doing with my girl, you old buzzard——?"

In the last dozen years, like most men in (knock-on-wood) fairly good health, I have had a few crushes and a few dates, and I even imagined myself in love. But fortunately or unfortunately, I have not been loved in return enough to bust anyone's heart or to make the awful mistake of attempting marriage at my time of life and for my kind of guy. Therefore, knowing this, and more important, feeling it all over, "I have loved lightly and in self-defense."

Some time ago, I met the brilliant young soprano Marion Marlowe. We dined together exactly twice, and outside of watching her on TV, I have not seen her since— But there were pictures printed of us in over one hundred papers.

When I became a bachelor in 1943, I did my best to act like I didn't care, with stunts like calling on a young lady at her apartment in New York in an old-fashioned hansom cab, driving it myself, and taking her around Central Park. The lady thought that was awfully funny, and that I certainly was a carefree cuss, until after the first trip around the park, I gave the driver his high hat and whip, and then cried on the young lady's shoulder because I was carrying a little torch—and she was most sympathetic. This young lady was a singer at the Copacabana in New York. Since then she has become a big star, both in England and on the Broadway stage, and has now entered the motion pictures in starring roles for MGM. She is a wonderful girl. Her name is Dolores Gray.

Little June Haver, now the wife of my friend Fred Mac-

Murray, is actually the only protégée I can claim, or that I can say I helped make a star of, since that morning in Chicago, at a motion picture theater when I presented a little girl by the name of Frances Gumm, and whispered in her ear just before she went on, "Child, forget your own name. You are now Judy Garland." I had great faith in lovely Miss Haver, so that I wrote most of and produced her first starring vehicle for the screen, *I Wonder Who's Kissing Her Now*.

I often dined and danced with Elizabeth "Cookie" Gordon, a gorgeous brunette who listens like an angel to anecdotes, poetry, and stories she has heard before, and then very sweetly says good night.

The other night, at a party given by Miss Sonja Henie, at which some two hundred people were present, I came alone and was seated at a table next to Marie MacDonald (Mrs. Harry Karl), and while dancing I spoke to her about her husband and what a great fellow he was, and that I hoped their current little differences would be patched. Toward the end of the evening she asked me would I drive downtown with her, as she wanted to talk to Miss Gloria de Haven, who was appearing at the Mocambo. I did, and Miss de Haven asked would I, on my way home, show her the way to get to the Sonja Henie party, as she was to meet Mr. Jeff Chandler (whom I once introduced in the following manner: "That fine actor, Jeff Chandler, who incidentally is the only full-blooded Jewish Indian Chief in the world . . ."). Mrs. Karl went home in her own car—Miss de Haven followed me in hers to Sonja's—I brought her to the door, took her right to Jeff, then had a nightcap, and went home alone. The following day, the newspapers had me dating both girls—which I certainly would like to do, had they been fancy-free, and if they had any feeling toward me other than I am a nice middle-aged gentleman who is so funny in conversation.

I have dined and danced with ever so many Hollywood lovelies. Those dancing by would see a look in my eyes as if I were swooning with love or something. My eyes give this impression for the following reasons: First, they have always watered a little since I was hit by a ball some years ago; secondly, my thoughts might be on a speech that I am working on about an old friend who is sick and near the finish; and thirdly, nearly all middle-aged people of my oriental ancestry are ready to cry at the drop of anything . . .

I believe I've called the ever-beauteous Joan Crawford on the phone almost as many times as I used to call my mother on the vaudeville stage. Miss Crawford is always so sweet, but is always either busy or has a date with somebody else . . .

And sometimes, sitting in a corner at a party with Barbara Stanwyck, I talked at great length to her, and she to me—about Al Jolson.

When Marilyn Monroe first came to Twentieth Century-Fox Studios—long before she became Mrs. Di Maggio—I was her escort to, I believe, the first stylish party she ever attended. She was just starting her career, and that is all she thought of and talked about. I remember that evening so well, because she was dressed in a maroon velvet gown that had come out of the studio. As she walked in, every eye turned toward her, from Henry Ford and his Mrs., for whom the party was given, every star in Hollywood, down to one particular busboy who dropped a tray every time he came anywhere near her.

I know a big beautiful blonde girl in New York called Barbara—and I know a big beautiful blonde girl in San Francisco called Barbara . . . and last year, in Paris, at Fouquets, a street café in the shadow of the Arc de Triomphe, I had coffee with Marlene Dietrich—just coffee.

And that makes up a dozen lovelies in a dozen years. I may have met many more girls—I can't seem to remember, and I bet they don't, either!

> And there will be no more Mocambo
>   swaying hip to hip
> And there'll be no honeyed murmurs
>   in a parked car on the Strip.
> Tho' the stars above are many
>   even more than MGM,
> Such carryings on belong to youth,
>   such nights are staged for them . . .
>
> *(with apologies to a more*
> *stylish "George": Lord Byron)*

Dear Jeri, when I visited you last week, I took a good look at your little bedroom, and having been warned in advance that it would look like Hurricane Helga had struck it, and knowing that nearly all little girls and boys, after a hard day at school and at play—and then again, reading about Scarlett O'Hara—throw their clothes on the floor and fall into bed, I was not at all surprised to find, on your dressing table, bobby pins in the cold-cream jar, a hairbrush in one of your shoes, and a complete mish-mosh all over.

I was happy to see, however, a picture of President Harry Truman still standing unscathed on the table, and I know that you will remember the incident when we went to visit him, and his secretary, Matt Connelly, brought you in first and left me standing outside for about a count of three. The president asked you, "Do you think I am as good-looking as your father?" and gave you a portrait of himself. Then, he sat you on his knee and gave you a little box, and inside it was a pencil on which was inscribed: "You swiped this from Harry Truman's desk." Incidentally, I have that pencil and am keeping it for you, as there is no need for that also to be stuck in the cold-cream jar with the bobby pins . . .

So, here's some more that you should know about Light-horse Harry:

21. Seen with the President

THE ASSIGNMENT that brought Harry Truman world fame was, in my opinion, the hardest that any man in public life had before him. For only a singer of popular songs, who has ever gone on the stage after Al Jolson finished singing, would have any idea what it was to follow Franklin D. Roosevelt in the presidency—for had Harry S. Truman entered the White House after either Mr. Coolidge or Mr. Hoover, he would have been looked upon as a dynamic personality. But he came in after Mr. Roosevelt, and this was something else again. Yet, strange as it may seem, in most places of the world he is now getting the bigger billing and louder world applause.

This friendship that I am so proud of became one of great affection during the presidential campaign of 1948. Before that I had known Mr. Truman only casually and had had private conversations with him only twice, the second occurred after a banquet following the last Inaugural of Mr. Roosevelt's, when Harry S. Truman became vice-president. I had been the Toastmaster on that occasion and had been bested in a battle of wits by Mrs. Roosevelt. During my speech in welcoming the audience of senators, congressmen, their wives, and other guests, I said something to this effect:

"We are beginning the speeches much earlier than we had planned, and I knew this would happen, because I knew you would all rush to the tables, because most of you, having had lunch at the White House today, had to be very, very hungry . . . I too lunched there—never in my life have I seen so much lettuce surrounding so little chicken . . . and while I know that the First Lady of the Land is so apt in so many things, if the chicken salad is any sign at all, she is not a very good cook."

A little later on, when I presented Mrs. Roosevelt, she topped me with: "I am sure Georgie is mistaken— I don't remember putting any chicken in the chicken salad . . ."

After the dinner was over, some of us had the extra cup of coffee in an anteroom—General Marshall, General Bradley, their wives, Mr. and Mrs. Truman, Fred Vinson, and some other Democrats. Mr. Truman and I talked about Kansas City, the old Orpheum there, the Lehmans—father and son —who managed the theater, the old Edwards Hotel. He sat down at the piano, and I told him about my reviving the song, "I'm Always Chasing Rainbows" in one of my pictures —and then he played a little bit of the Chopin melody from which the song was taken, and that was that.

It was some time before I saw him again, and it came about in this manner:

A good friend of mine, Bryan Foy—popular picture producer *par excellence* and elder son of the illustrious Eddie Foy—called me on the phone.

"Georgie," he said, "so-and-so, whom you like very much, took the rap for some fellows higher up, and as you know has paid his debt to society. He is on parole, and what he deserves is a clean bill of health."

I agreed. "What can I do about it, Brynie?" I said.

"Well, we got to do something before the election. Much as I don't want it to happen, it looks like the Republicans will have a cinch, and I don't know any of them well enough to ask whether they can help our friend. So maybe, Georgie, you can join this Democratic Committee with me, make a few speeches, and some big shot might help us with our problem. Of course, so-and-so is such a nice fellow, and he did get a bad deal."

I said, "Okay. Let me know what you want me to do."

A few days later there appeared in the Los Angeles *Herald Express* an item which said that Mr. Truman was coming to California to make some speeches and that I would introduce him at the baseball park, Gilmore Field, in Hollywood. I was called in by one of the men in high office at Twentieth Century-Fox Studios where I was a producer.

The man said, "Georgie, your politics belong to you, but be sure that in whatever speeches you make, you don't give the impression that you are speaking for our company, as we have so many Republicans. Anyway, do you think that Truman and the Democrats have a chance?"

And I said, "I don't——"

Then he said, "Why get yourself mixed up in something, when you can't win . . . etc., etc."

I thought it over and made up my mind he was perfectly right, and I wrote a letter to the newspaper and said I had not been asked to introduce Mr. Truman by anyone who had such authority, and that while I would deem it a privilege to meet Mr. Truman in California, I also would be happy to meet Governor Dewey of New York, and would be honored to shake their hands, not as candidates for further office but just to renew acquaintances, in respect for the offices they held.

About a month or two later Mr. Truman did come to California. I received another phone call from Brynie Foy, saying that he had met the president in San Francisco and that Mr. Truman had asked for me. This I didn't believe!

Later on I received a message from Helen Gahagan Douglas, repeating what Foy had said. This, too, I didn't believe; I figured Foy had told Helen. And then one morning there was a phone call from Truman's secretary, a wonderful fellow in or out of high office, Matt Connelly, in the course of which he said the president wanted to see me.

I went down to the Biltmore Hotel, expecting to stand in line and shake hands along with a group of a few loyal Democrats—hardly any from the theatrical profession, with the exception of Ronald Reagan, the Bogarts, and one or two others. But instead I was taken to meet Mr. Truman alone, and he said, "I want you to be with me tonight and say a few words, if you will."

Mr. Truman had been through and was still going through the hottest baptismal fire that any candidate has ever experienced because he was doing it single-handed throughout most of the country, getting help from very few, with the exception of the noblest Kentuckian of them all, Alben Barkley, who was campaigning in the East. Mr. Truman's voice was almost gone. I was later told that with almost every sentence he uttered, he would look toward his wife and then his daughter Margaret as if to ask, "Are they hearing me?"

In reply to his request I said to him, "Mr. President, I am very honored that you should ask for me, but I know little of politics out here in California, and am particularly ignorant of the state issues, and I don't think I can be of much help, for surely this is too tense a campaign to inject any comic relief or light banter, which is about all I would have to offer."

"Well," he said, "come on up with me anyway."

About fifty of us had dinner, and then a committeeman called our names and told us what number car to take to drive out and make some sort of a little parade to escort the president to Gilmore Field. I was called last and told to wait, that I would ride with the president.

We entered an open car, with a chauffeur and Secret Service man in front, Mr. Truman and I. The streets were not crowded, even though it had been announced in the one impartial paper that the president would drive up the main highway to the ball park. About every three or four blocks a voice would be heard, "I think you can do it!" or "Give them hell, Harry!" and that is about all the enthusiasm that was prevalent. And Mr. Truman would answer and wave his hand to whoever shouted at him.

We talked on the way about Roosevelt, and while being thoroughly respectful I tried to console Mr. Truman about the election, which I was sure he would lose. I spoke of the fact of how proud his old mother must be to have reached this fine old age and to have seen her son go to such great heights. I told Mr. Truman that posterity would surely favor him and particularly for what he had done in respect to the American Negro, and that no one else, including Mr. Roosevelt and all other presidents before him put together, had given anything but lip service since Mr. Abraham Lincoln.

At one corner we encountered a little crowd and Mr. Truman beamed, and I talked to him about street popularity— how little it amounted to—about how once, when I was interested in a play that Jack Dempsey appeared in, thousands of people came to meet him at the depot, but very few came to buy tickets for the show. And how even to the last the crowd would follow Jimmy Walker through the streets of New York and ask for his autograph, but so few would give him a job.

We arrived at Gilmore Field, and in speaking for the president I said only the following:

"I am happy to be in so close proximity to the man who

holds the highest office in the greatest land . . ." and in a few words told the audience, more than half of which were Negro, what I had told the president in the car. I summed it up by saying: "No other man in his position has so stuck his chin out to help any minority as Harry S. Truman."

This might not sound like anything much, but it got a lot of applause. The president made a speech and introduced his Bess and his Margaret; it all seemed very homey—but it just did not seem enough, I thought.

We rode down to the depot; we had a drink and another chat. I put my arms around him before I left and said I knew that the Lord would continue to bless him, and said good-by.

And then, contrary to the opinions of about ninety per cent of the newspapers, and all the wise-acres, he was elected, and though I had only had this tiniest of association in the campaign, Mr. Truman never forgot it and has not to this day.

During his administration and since his retirement, we have seen each other frequently. On almost every occasion in Washington on which he was to appear, the president would request me to be there. (The closest I've been to Washington during this present administration is Baltimore.)

On one occasion, at the White House Photographers' Dinner, I remember introducing the brilliant young pianist André Previn in this manner: I brought him up on the stage and said, "I am sure you realize, young man, that this is quite an occasion for you to play before such an illustrious audience—and during your career you may not always find such a warm reception as I know you will receive here. But come what may, be of good cheer—for who knows how far you may go. Look what has happened to another piano player!"

On another occasion, at a dinner for Secretary of the Treasury John Snyder, I introduced Mr. Truman and he made an address, reading from a manuscript that had been contrived for the radio. When it was over and he was off the air, I turned to his aide and said, "I wish the president would speak without script to this group, as I know they would like to hear him." This conversation went on while the audience was still applauding. I was told that the president had not prepared anything else and that that was that. However, I arose quickly and said, "I am sure the president will pardon me, but I live in California and only get this close to him once in a while. I know that you feel, as I do, that you would like to have him talk to us a little bit more intimately than he did in his radio address. I am sure that I am not impertinent in asking him to speak again, and if I am, I don't know what he could do to me. I cannot be deported, I am an American—my father, my mother, and my grandmother were born in New York—and you can't go much further back than that unless your aunt was Pocahontas."

The president arose and started with this line, "Georgie Jessel must be very tired, because he would rather listen to himself."

These days, when he comes to New York, I often meet Mr. Truman a little before 7 A.M. and walk with him. He is followed and cheered by crowds of people as he goes through the streets—more and more people each time he comes to New York, and more and more cheers.

In 1950, I came to see him with a plan to build a national theater in the city of Washington. It seemed such a pity that this, the most prosperous country in the world, not only has no national theater but no real theater of any kind in the capitol of the world, where great attractions or great spectacles can play. Even the smallest cities in Europe have a great theater that they can point to with pride. The idea as to how it would be run appeared in the press as follows:

TRUMAN ENTHUSES AS JESSEL OUTLINES
HIS NATIONAL THEATER

"Washington, June 1. Georgie Jessel, who came here to speak before the Atlantic Union Committee convention tomorrow, pow-wowed with President Truman today about a national theater project. He emerged, bubbling with enthusiasm, and told *Daily Variety* the president indicated belief the government would accept a national theater, such as envisioned by Jessel, if it were gifted by a group of private citizens.

"Jessel's chief reason for visit was to determine whether government could and would accept a theater to run as a national project. His plans call for a $3,000,000.00 auditorium which would house not only legit, operas, ballets, etc., but quasi-official patriotic shows which now go begging for a site.

"Jessel said Philadelphia publisher Walter Annenberg, and Blevins Davis, personal friend of the president and angel of many art productions, were among those willing to finance the idea. Vet showman added that such a project would become government property only after it paid back original investors. It would then be operated on a self-sustaining basis as a 'theater run by showmen who know show business.'

"Jessel plans to enlist top showbiz names in a campaign for the idea."

However, I stressed the fact that this theater should be owned by the government under the direction of a showman, and as government property it would strengthen democracy and break down some old-fashioned thinking in the city of Washington itself. I wanted to call it the American Theatre, and like the post office where the American Negro can walk in and buy a stamp, so could he walk into the American Theater and buy a ticket. Mr. Truman was all for it and suggested that such a theater should be called Roosevelt Memorial Theater. Nothing ever came of it. Congress turned it down. Perhaps I'll try it again when a new administration comes into power.

But of all of the things that have happened to me during the last dozen years, the warmest and most important pat on the back I'll ever have is when Mr. Truman, at a public dinner in Washington, said, "As President of the United States, I would like to present to you the Toastmaster General of our country, Georgie Jessel."

The warmest memory of all in my association with Mr. Truman was when I went down to the east side of New York during the Stevenson campaign and presented him to a quarter of a million people in the shadow of the Williamsburg Bridge—and what was formerly called the Ghetto looked as spic and span as anything that ever your eyes have seen. Old people cried as the president spoke; they had never been so close to a great man who was also a warm friend. Never before did any president come so far downtown to talk to these people.

When he finished, I said, "Now I know what his middle initial stands for— The S is for Solomon!"

Well, kid, remember the fun we had down at my house at the beach when you brought down your little pals Sharon and Susan? We played catch, and your lefty pitching found the ball in the pool or over the fence most of the time. Then, it got foggy, and we went inside, played the phonograph, and later watched the ball game on TV.

This was a Saturday, I recall, so while all this was going on, I brought out my little radio to hear the results on the horse races. There was no real reason for me to do this, except that I had bet on every race, and so that I won't be investigated for this terrible crime, I must explain that these bets were made by Cousin Milford who had gone to the race track to place them.

And so, here are some notes about all the things we did that day:—music, the national pastime, the sport of kings, and others.

22. Caruso, McGraw, and Mays

IN THE ever-quick-changing picture of things in our time, the opera has been in the foreground, and the walls of the Metropolitan have heard some mighty strange sounds lately.

I acquired a great love for the opera at a very early age. I recall my father having a surprise for me when I was six: a Victor phonograph. First I heard the music, and then he took me into the living room and showed me the machine. It was a recording of Enrico Caruso singing the aria *Spirito*

Gentile from *La Favorita.* This was followed by several records which included the voices of Di Gorgoza, Caruso, Melba, Destinn, Scotti, and others.

By the time I was nine, I was acquainted with the music of nearly all of the Italian and French operatic composers and conversant with nearly every important aria in their works.

And then, as I entered the show business, I managed at every opportunity to go to the Met. Two dollars out of the fifteen I was earning from Gus Edwards would take me into the gallery or let me stand at the back, and often a kindly disposed gentleman standing next to me would lift me up when Caruso sang Rodolfo's narrative in *La Bohème* or *"Lucevan le Stelle"* from *Tosca.*

The impresario of the Met was Heinrich Conried, and soon after, Gatti-Casazza took his place. Through the years that followed, I became personally acquainted with many of the opera stars, and as I earned more money as an actor, I kept buying a seat closer to the stage.

I was present at many eventful occasions: the last performance of Geraldine Farrar—a matinée—where, after the final curtain fell, the audience cheered and threw roses on the stage until it was time for the night performance to begin. I saw the first performance of Jeritza in *Totte Stadt (The Dead City)* by Korngold. On one Saturday night I heard a packed Met audience join the cast in weeping, when after the second act of *La Bohème* the ushers walked down the aisle with pamphlets which carried the news that Puccini had died. At the end of the performance the orchestra played Gounod's Funeral March.

And so, on through the years: From Chaliapin to Pinza, to the present-day Siepi, from De Luca, Scotti to Bob Merrill, from Caruso, Martinelli, Gigli, to Bjoerling and the two

great recruits from temples and synagogues, Jan Peerce and
Richard Tucker—from Melba, Nordica, Alda, Muzio, to Bori,
Ponselle, Galli-Curci, Pons, to little Roberta Peters. Even the
Chicago Opera could not escape me: Rosa Raisa, Rimini,
George Baclanov, Tito Schipa, who made me the godfather
of his little girl.

And as a kid I listened wide-eyed to the conversations of
the great operatic feud between Oscar Hammerstein the
first, and the tycoons who backed the Met. Hammerstein,
with the courage of Marciano, Liberace, and little David
of the Bible, built the Manhattan Opera House in New York.
He personally brought back with him from Europe the beautiful Lina Cavalieri, soprano, and tenors Muratore and Ales-
sandro Bonci. He tried every trick of the showman during
his short time as an operatic impresario (they bought him
out quickly). He took the Irish concert singer, John McCormack and introduced him to opera in *Martha;* he produced
the opera *Thaïs* and instead of just having the orchestra play
the "Meditation," a spotlight was thrown on the first violinist
who happened to be the great Mischa Elman. And unless
my memory fails me, Hammerstein was first to bring out one
who was known as one of the first American prima donnas,
Mary Garden . . . for until lately, with the exception of Garden, Ponselle, and little Miss Marian Talley, there were few
American opera singers at the Met: the few ladies I've mentioned, and the tenors Orville Harold and Richard Crooks.
Harold was knocked off quickly after a season of Richard
Wagner, while he should have been singing from Puccini,
Massenet, and Donizetti's *Una Furtiva Lacrima.* Crooks re-
turned to the concert stage and the Victor Company.

The dearth of American voices was so evident that I used
to tell this story (and I still do) about how a young American soprano was given a chance to sing the role of Aïda.

This opportunity came to her after singing Musetta in *La Bohème* for eight years. Anyway, at the dress rehearsal in full costume, she showed herself in front of the impresario and said, "How do I look?" and the maestro said, "There's something very wrong. Aïda, you must know, is a voluptuous princess, and you don't look it, because you have no bust." "But," answered the girl, "the curtain goes up in but a few hours, and I doubt whether I can develop in time . . ." "Oh, this is very simple," said the impresario, "Just go down to the property room, and ask the master property man to give you some Aïda busts—I am sure we have them . . ." A few moments later she came up wearing around her bosom something that looked like two barrels of flour. "Is that what you want?" said the girl. "Good Lord, no!" the impresario exclaimed, "they made a mistake—they've given you Falstaff's behind."

Since then, of course, and because of the fact that wars in Europe have curtailed the activity of opera, particularly in Italy, American singers have been given quite a chance and have not been lacking in voices. Then, after the resignation of Edward Johnson, the Met turned itself over and placed its destiny in the hands of Rudolf Bing, a highly talented and therefore highly touted impresario from somewhere around Vienna, who has done some wonderful things and also some awful things—but he is to be saluted at all times for trying. I thought his production of *Faust*, bringing it up a few hundred years as far as costume and locale is concerned, was good showmanship. I believe his plan for opening the 1954-55 season with a potpourri of scenes from the great operas with an all-star cast, was wonderful. There are two or three things, however, that have had him out on a limb. For example, first, the production of *Pagliacci*. As most of you know, the opera begins with a prologue in which Tonio, dressed as a circus clown, comes in front of the curtain and tells the story of the play, and what the author has intended. This, since its inception, has been sung with the singer almost leaning over the orchestra, as if to say, "This is what is going to go on" and as if he were telling every member of the audience personally. For some strange reason in the last Bing production of *Pagliacci* the prologue singer was dressed in a Mexican sombrero and placed almost at the back of the stage, and then, when the curtain rose, instead of seeing the familiar and honest setting of the little Italian village readying itself for the circus, there was a big stick on the stage, as if placed in the middle of a drum . . . and to be perfectly frank, I don't know to this day what it was. I only know that in order to enjoy *Pagliacci* from then on, you had to just close your eyes and listen to the music, for, if you opened them, you might find Johnnie Ray lying on the floor in tears—but even Johnnie could never weep as much as I am sure Leoncavallo would have if he had witnessed this particular production of his great dramatic and musical creation.

The next thing was an opera called *The Rake* in which the settings after Hogarth were just wonderful, the English libretto articulate, but the recitative music abominable. I sat with my friend S. Hurok, and despite the fact that he loves everybody, he kept hitting me with his cane all through the second act. It is hard to believe that Stravinsky, composer of the wonderful *Firebird*, raked this thing up. Melodically, it was like hearing your best friend wretching.

That particular season also presented a great challenge to Mr. Bing: the performance of *La Bohème* in English. And while the lyricist Howard Dietz did a good job and the movie director Joseph Mankiewicz made the action more realistic and stopped Barcoloni from eating the scenery, even beautiful *La Bohème* cannot stand being translated. For it is the music at all times in opera, and particularly the running-brook melody of *La Bohème*. Through the years we have listened to the notes, and no matter how badly the actor or actress may speak or sing the Italian language, it makes no difference if the voices are good, and 99,999 people out of a 100,000 would not be offended if there were a grammatical error throughout a clear, high B-flat . . . but brother, when it is in English, and in a dialect, a mispronounced word or an unrealistic one is just murder.

There's an aria in *Aïda* in which there are practically just about two words: "*Mai pui, mai pui* . . .," and not knowing what *Mai pui* means, it makes no difference if it is sung beautifully. But if the two words are "no more" or "why not" or some such thing, after sixteen bars you want to shoot yourself. There are just some certain things that cannot be changed into English. They just lose everything. Certain French, Irish, or Yiddish stories should be left untold, unless they can be rendered as they were originally intended.

Next to Italian opera, beautiful things that suffer most by translation into English are the ancient Hebrew chants, as well as many of the fervent prayers. The sacred song of the *Kol Nidrei* sung on the eve of the Day of Atonement, makes Jew or non-Jew alike touched by it. In English it is as effective as a marshmallow on a football field.

I am sure Maestro Bing agrees with me. There are some things that can't be changed, even though we think they can. You all know the story of the famous banker, Otto Kahn. Whether it is true or not, I don't know, but it goes like this:

Kahn was walking down Fifth Avenue with a famous wit of his time whose name was Marshall P. Wilder. Wilder was a little hunchback, but he overcame this physical defect by his fine mind and great literate sense of humor. He and Kahn passed a famous church. "Marshall," Kahn said, "this is my church. I am one of the pillars of it." Wilder said, "Why, Mr. Kahn, I thought you were a Jew," and Mr. Kahn supposedly answered, "I changed." After walking five more minutes, Marshall suddenly said, "You know, I used to be a hunchback."

In 1910, I was a batboy at the Polo Grounds chasing bats and doing errands for the New York Giants, who were then under the iron guidance of John J. McGraw. Those high in the public eye at that time were Christy Mathewson, affectionately called Matty, and I believe it was either Bozman Bolger or Hype Igoe who called him Big Six, and a lot of the fans followed suit.

Matty was a big, handsome, blond man, and were he the star Giant pitcher of today, Hollywood and TV would have taken him off the pitcher's box even quicker than Durocher puts Wilhelm in to pitch. However, the only association with the amusement world that Matty had was a two-week engagement at Hammerstein's Victoria Theatre on 42nd Street, in which he played a sketch assisted by his battery mate, the Big Indian, Chief Meyers.

Of all the Giant players I can only recall two others who ever went on the stage. They were the hard-hitting outfielder Mike Donlin, who also later became a picture actor, and the lanky pitcher Rube Marquard. Both Donlin and Marquard were married to highly talented actresses: Donlin to the comedienne Mabel Hite, and Marquard to the great song stylist Blossom Seeley.

When the Giants won the game, I would follow them to their dressing room, and while they were showering, I would sing popular songs. Sometimes we would form a quartet:

Matty, myself, Larry Doyle, the second baseman, and little Brownie, who was my pal and assistant bat chaser. And then, as the players were leaving the club, they would throw me some change and I split it with Brownie. But if the Giants lost, I would have to go to the visiting club, as there was no singing in the clubhouse when McGraw's lads lost a ball game. I remember trying it once, and Mugsie, as McGraw was unaffectionately called by some, would say, "Get out of here, you little——. You're bad luck." But the following day it would all be forgotten, if the Giants won!

The baseball greats of that time were Ty Cobb, with Detroit and the eccentric Rube Waddell, although he was finishing his career. He made conversation in all sports circles in the same manner as Buggs Raymond and Dizzy Dean did later on. But of Waddell, there was the never-to-be-forgotten incident of the time he was called in to pitch with no one out and three men on base for the opposing team. He called the outfielders in and told them to sit down on the bench, and he struck the next three batters out.

The trio of Tinkers to Evers to Chance was the famous Chicago Cubs infield sensation, and Connie Mack, manager of the Philadelphia Athletics, was baseball's master mind and its most beloved figure. Incidentally, I have given but two dinner parties in the ten years that I have lived in my Santa Monica Beach home—one was in honor of Greer Garson, never lovelier, and the other to Connie Mack, nearly ninety.

Now, in our time, the baseball scene has changed like everything else. Only the very fittest of the teams can survive, the minor leagues are swiftly going where vaudeville went, and it is only the leading clubs in the major leagues or a new entry, such as Milwaukee or Baltimore, that do any business. Even the most ardent baseball fans stay home and watch it on TV, and although this is a godsend for people who have to remain in, it never can compare to the thrill of being actually at the ball park, where you can see every play, and not just a close-up of one or two plays.

I think the most nerve-shattering and hardest job that a man can have is to be manager of a ball team; and unless you have been awfully close to ball players and intimately know a manager or two, it is almost impossible to believe what they go through. They are respected or disrespected with every play of the game. The manager takes a pitcher out and the opposing batter gets a hit off the new pitcher. The manager is a bum. If the new pitcher strikes out the opposing batter, the manager knew just when to put him in. The same with a pinch-hitter and with every play that is made. If he is a playing manager, it is much worse, for when he himself fails to do what he has told any one of his men, or should he make the same fumble that he raised hell with one of his players for doing, he might just as well quit. The manager, when I was a kid, had a much easier time, for he ran the ball club. Nowadays he doesn't. Every team has a front-office general manager, and these gentlemen seem to be getting more authority all the time, so that with the slightest sign of friction between general manager and the field manager, the entire morale of the ball club goes to pieces. And even though Leo Durocher, of the Giants, has done such a wonderful job in winning the pennant with a team that does not look like it can do so on paper, today's daily papers claim there is trouble between him and the front office. This front-office business sells an awful lot of ulcer medicine to baseball managers.

An incident that brings out how very seriously baseball men take their profession occurred a couple of years ago, with a meeting of my daughter Jerilynn and Branch Rickey. Mr. Rickey is probably the greatest impresario or general baseball mind of our times, and his memory will be kept ever green with the fact that his was the first team to bring a Negro ball player to the major leagues: Jackie Robinson. Since then all racial bans in baseball have been torn down, and this has been not only for the good of the game, but more important, for the good of democracy and America.

In the last few years, through Bob Cobb of the Hollywood team and Fred Haney, manager of the Pittsburgh team, Mr. Rickey and I have become warm friends. And so one day I brought Jerilynn in to meet him. I said, "Jeri, I want you to meet Branch Rickey, one of the greatest men in baseball." And Rickey, a man of seventy, said to her, "My child, you don't want to meet me now. My team is in last place. You wait a couple of years and I'll make you proud of me." In other words, despite Rickey's greatness, he considered himself unworthy of praise because on that particular day his club was in last place.

In no other business is there so much criticism as there is in baseball. TV shows can be panned once a week; a motion picture actor may be knocked five or six times throughout the year; a dramatic author a dozen times in ten years. But the baseball man has to get the early edition of the papers every day, from April to September, year in year out, and read whether he's a bum or a hero, whether he's at his peak or at the finish. The ball player has to take abuse like no other public figure in the world. The distance between the grandstand and the bleachers from the playing field is not very large. But it seems to give the spectator the right to heap any sort of insult he can think of on the ball player, and get away with it. Some years ago, when Leo Durocher was banished from baseball for a short time because of striking a spectator under the grandstand after the game, I was asked by Vincent O'Flaherty, the sports writer of the Los Angeles *Examiner,* for my opinion on the incident. I wrote an editorial on it, which appeared in Mr. O'Flaherty's column and others, and I interceded for Leo with my good friend Happy Chandler (then head of baseball), but this is how the Durocher incident came about:

A ball player under Leo's management had gone through the pangs of having his wife leave him unexpectedly. It naturally affected him on the ball field. This incident had been in the papers, and a spectator started to ride or heckle him every time he came to bat, yelling at him, "You're a bum —no wonder your wife left you." Leo found out where the man was sitting and tried to get him to stop, but could not and so he waited for him and hit him, and the man deserved it. In my newspaper piece I wrote of a conversation I had heard once in the New York subway. Two kids were talking. One said, "I hate my boss, and some day I'm going to call him an s.o.b." "How are you going to do that?" said the other kid. The first one said, "It's easy—I'll sit behind him when he goes to the ball game, and I'll holler 'you dirty s.o.b.,' and if he turns around, I'll say I was just saying it to one of the ball players. Everybody is allowed to do that!"

Yes, the life of a ball player is a hard life. A hit in the head, and you not only are through with baseball but through with life; a broken leg or arm, and you got to find a new business; if you should have ten good years, you can't spread the taxes out, despite the fact that your earning capacity may be practically nil after that time—unless you are like the few who can make the grade and become managers . . . and that's even worse than the taxes.

I don't approve of umpire-baiting. I think it is terribly silly to keep fighting over a decision that an umpire makes that can't be changed. But because of the tension that the ball player is under continuously, there must be some tolerance. Out on the Coast League, the Hollywood Club has a fiery little base stealer called Carlos Bernier. He lost his head completely and last year hit an umpire and was deservedly taken out of baseball for a year or more. And there was no defense for Carlos, although to give the incident a little comedy relief, I made an address at the ball park while presenting an award to the popular Hollywood outfielder Frank Keleher. I was wearing the baseball uniform of Carlos Bernier. I told that to the audience and said that while I couldn't condone Carlos' act, I understood that he had slapped the umpire because he was not conversant with the English language . . . that Bernier came from a little island near Portugal in which they spoke a language violently different from English and that in Carlos' native tongue, the words "You're out," used by the umpire, had an entirely different meaning and to Carlos it sounded like "Your sister is an awful flirt!" And for that reason Carlos lost his head.

Yes, it's tough being a ball player, and if you think it's easy, just reach up to catch a foul ball some day that comes your way in the grandstand or the bleachers—and if the ball contacts you, please give your business to my dear friend Dr. Blaustein: Lackawanna 4-0870.

For fear of giving any idea that I think I am a hot shot about sports in general, let me first say that I know a little bit only about baseball, the fight ring, and enough about racing not to bet too much. I know absolutely nothing of football, having seen only one game and a half; I have never seen a hockey match or any of the other sports.

New York kids all took to baseball because they could throw a ball or play catch in their back yards, or on the streets between Ehretz beer wagons going by. Also you could buy a baseball for a nickel, and there was very little thought of the kids where I came from ever going to Harvard or Yale and learning to play football.

We kids also took to prizefighting because of the colorful fighters' pictures that used to go with little candy bars we bought for a penny. And there was always a picture or two of some fighter in the saloons of our neighborhood, which we used to admire when our elders would take us along for a bite of free lunch while they had their beer can filled for a dime.

And so, although I now meet the boys who don the big gloves at Toots Shor's, I first met them as a kid at Billy Gibson's place in the Bronx—and even before that, when as a song plugger, I would be around 14th Street and venture into Tom Sharkey's saloon with Joe Cooper.

I have known Corbett, Jack Johnson, Jeffries, Dempsey, Gene Tunney, Joe Louis, Max Baer, and Jimmie Braddock, and Carnera—and just a short time ago I did a TV show with the present champion Rocky Marciano.

I think Dempsey at his best was the greatest heavyweight of them all. I think Joe Louis would have knocked him down, but I think he would have got up fighting, as he did when Firpo knocked him out of the ring.

I think the present champion, Rocky Marciano, would have given Dempsey his best fight. Rocky has no idea of blood or pain, but with Dempsey, I think the referee would have had to stop it if Rocky were cut up too much, although Marciano would still want to come out fighting.

The bantam and featherweight fighters are not talked about much these days. The last thing I heard about a bantam match was somewhere in the deep Orient, where a Frenchman called Robert Cohen defended his title successfully, and the only reason why I saw this is because I was attracted by the headline,

COHEN KEEPS TITLE

The lightweights and middleweights of today I don't think compare with those who were in the ring when I was Jerilynn's age. There is nobody around with the tenacity of Battling Nelson, or the skill of Joe Gans or Packy MacFarland or Abe Attell . . . and Benny Leonard had the virtues of all these. There is no welterweight around like Mickey Walker, and certainly no light-heavyweights like Georges Carpentier and Harry Greb. And there is no welterweight or one hundred thirty-eight-pound lightweights around like Barney Ross, Henry Armstrong, and Jimmy McLarnin.

In fact, most people who have any knowledge of boxing because of TV don't even know the fighter's name when they tune in a little late, and if you ask who is fighting, they say, "It's a ten-round match between Pabst Blue Ribbon and How Are You Fixed For Blades?"

I'll say very little about the races, as I go so few times and generally lose the money I've allotted myself to bet around the fourth race—but I've been to race tracks all over America, and all over Europe, and I believe racing is better now than ever before. It has become more individualistic, for in the old days the better horses ran on a fast track and also in the goo. Today they don't. And while no one horse is as good as Man O'War, I think that most of them are better than the competition in his time. The starting gate is a thousand times more accurate than the barrier, and the eye of the camera tells the true story of a close finish.

Racing in England has improved a little bit, but in France

it stays the same. The races are much longer than ours, and they start ad lib out of sight. Sometimes, after the first mile, they ride behind tall trees, and one afternoon at St. Cloud I could swear a couple of the boys had changed their colors and one jockey was smoking a pipe. Then, after the race is over, it seems to take at least an hour and a half to decide the mutuels.

As to the riders, I never saw Isaac Murphy or Tod Sloan (Cantor knew them both personally!), but I've seen and am fairly well acquainted with all of the present-day riders. The Jockeys' Guild, headed by Eddie Arcaro, Ted Atkinson, Headley Woodhouse, and others, presented me with their Guild's Award of Merit at a dinner at the Waldorf two years ago. I have also been the guest of the boys who ride out in California. I gave the Silver Saddle Award to Johnny Longden after this three thousandth victory at Hollywood Park, and I think Wee Willie Shoemaker can hold his own with all of them, including Sir Gordon Richards from England.

My closest pal, little Sammie Renick, who still looks like he did when he rode two-year-olds, is now on TV, where he tells the story of the big-stake races. He has become most articulate and is a fine performer, and I wouldn't be surprised if within a short time, he turned to the theater. You may some day see advertised in the Sunday New York *Times:* "The Theatre Guild, by arrangement with the Jockey Club, presents Mr. Samuel Renick in *Richard the Third.*"

Jerilynn, you are not far from your thirteenth birthday, and you think that someone who is twenty-nine is terribly old. The thought of anyone close to you being suddenly removed from this life never enters your mind. And these things are as they should be. Many years ago your father felt the same way; but in my late twenties, the theatrical profession began calling on me whenever there was a gathering of men for some purpose or other, particularly when I became the Abbot of the Friars and the president of the National Variety Artists, Vice-President of the Jewish Theatrical Guild, and other fraternal and charitable organizations.

It was then that I was called upon to speak at the passing of brother members of any of these organizations, particularly so if they were in the public eye. For the first few years this was more like a theatrical performance, but soon it became grim reality. Saying farewell publicly to a friend took time and great emotional toll.

With the passing of the years this toll has become almost unbearable, for I have had to speak too often, and I have to grit my teeth and hold my hands tightly to the pulpit in order to be able to carry on. For it has been my sad duty to speak at the biers of many men I have known all my life, and eulogize, even though some were not completely virtuous—and who is? Time, which is so often cruel, brings with it one wonderful gift in that it makes everything old seem sinless. And as Edgar Lee Masters has written, "One always forgives the blindness of the departed owl."

But most of the men about whom I have spoken were really dear to me, and there was not one whom I had not known for less than twenty years; George M. Cohan, John Barrymore, Al Jolson, Sam Harris, Will Rogers, William Morris, Jimmy Walker, Gus Edwards, Bert Kalmar, Sime Silverman, Ben Bernie,

George Gershwin, Sid Grauman, Samuel Hoffenstein,
Fannie Brice and others.

So, with the passing of people so well known, the
press and the radio used quotes and sometimes my en-
tire eulogy for the departed one. Perforce of this, I re-
ceived hundreds of letters asking for copies of what I
had said. As a courtesy to me, the Columbia Broad-
casting System sent out more than fifteen thousand
copies of the piece I spoke for Al Jolson. With this in
mind, I devote a chapter to some of the farewells. You
may find some repetitions, but there is no reason for
not repeating one line or two from Mary Baker Eddy,
or reciting the Twenty-Third Psalm of David.

23. Eulogy for Al Jolson.
Temple Israel
OCTOBER 26, 1950

A BREEZE FROM San Francisco Bay and the life
of the greatest minstrel America has ever known is in the
balance. A turn of a card—a telling of a gag—and within
a few moments, a wife, a legion of admirers, and a nation are
broken-hearted. So it was—and so, alas, it is—the passing
from this earthly scene of Al Jolson. And the voice that put
majesty into the American popular song must from now on
come from a disc instead of the heart, from whence it came.

Oh, my friends, I know it is the purpose of the speaker
at times like this to voice lofty phrases of consolation about
a life full lived and a happy conclusion to a great career.

But I, contemporary of Al's, find myself being too shocked and torn within to say that all is well, and I dare not lie from this sacred platform to say that I, and we, must rejoice in the fact that now he is at peace. It would be far from the truth, and I would need the spiritual strength of a rabbi, a minister, and a priest combined to do so. The human flesh and the frailty of human nature seem to be the sad order of the day as far as I am concerned.

It will take a long time for the people in my business who have been wounded by this event to become reconciled that this dynamic bundle of energy with its God-given talent that called itself Al Jolson is at peace. The very humanly emotional heart of the theatrical business does not heal so easily, and the tears that must fall from the eyes of the many who miss him already cannot be halted by the spoken word. No, the word will not take the place of his song.

And not only has the entertainment world lost its king, but we cannot cry, "The King is dead—long live the King!" For there is no one to hold his scepter. Those of us who tarry behind are but pale imitations, mere princelings. And American Jewry suffers as well—and I must psychologically inform you of the great inspiration that Al was to the Jewish people in the last forty years. For in 1910 the Jewish people who emigrated from Europe to come here were a sad lot. Their humor came out of their own troubles. Men of thirty-five seemed to take on the attitude of their fathers and grandfathers, they walked with stooped shoulders. When they sang, they sang with lament in their hearts and their voices, always as if they were pleading for help from above. And the older they got, the more they prayed for the return to Jerusalem. Or yearned for the simple little villages where they spent their childhood. And the actors, even the great ones, came on the stage also playing characters like their fathers. Vaudeville and the variety and the musical-comedy stage and the legitimate theater had Ben Welch and Joe Welch, monologists with beards and shabby clothes telling humorous stories that had a tear behind them. Likewise did this happen in legitimate theater. David Warfield in *The Auctioneer* and many others in plays bewailing the misfortunes that had happened to the Jew. And then there came on the scene a young man, vibrantly pulsing with life and courage, who marched on the stage, head high with the authority of a Roman emperor, with a gaiety that was militant, uninhibited, and unafraid, and told the world that the Jew in America did not only have to sing in sorrow but could shout happily about Dixie, about the Night Boat to Albany, about coming to California, about a girl in Avalon. And when he cried "Mammy" it was in appreciation, not in lament. Jolson is the happiest portrait that can ever be painted about an American of the Jewish faith. Jolson was synonymous with victory—at the race track, at the ball game, at anything that he participated in, he would say, "I had the winner, ha, ha, why didn't you ask me?" This was not in bravado alone: this was the quintessence of optimism. Whatever you're in, whatever game you play, feel like you are the winner.

The history of the world does not say enough about how important the song and the singer have been, from the days of old when a man first sang "Yankee Doodle" on the streets of Boston or the soldier in France who first sang "The Marseillaise." But history must record the name Jolson, who in the twilight of his life sang his heart out in a foreign land, to the wounded and to the valiant. I am proud to have basked in the sunlight of his greatness, to have been part of his time, and to have only a few days ago—this last Sunday night—hugged him and said, "Good night, Asa, take care of yourself." And now, my friends, I find my faith in good coming back to me. I feel strengthened in heart and mind—and I would lay my sackcloth and ashes aside and therefore say to my fellow mourners and the little lady who bears Al's name that I am thankful to God that there was and there is an Al Jolson. And I have faith that he will never die in the hearts of people. No, no. No such blot will ever fall on the fair charter of American memories. *Baruch adenoi,* Praise the Lord. Good night, Al.

Jeri darling, I think about the worst sound out-side of the cry of the wounded on the battlefield is that of older people making with baby talk, like, "Is oo dadda's iddie dolla baby," etc.

But once there was a fine gal who became a big star. However, before getting up to the top, she served full apprenticeship as chorus girl and singer in burlesque. She finally became one of the world's greatest come-diennes, and like all great comics, there was always the tragic side a breath away. She could make you laugh singing a song about being an Indian Jewess, and with one turn of your program, come back on stage, stand under a dimly lit lamp post, and break your heart sing-ing a lament about a cruel lover in "My Man."

But very late in her life most people remember her as Baby Snooks, which she played both on the stage and then for years on the radio. Snooks was a five-year-old child, a combination of Topsy, Peck's Bad Boy, and the Katzenjammer Kids—fictional characters, but mis-chievous though lovable youngsters.

Fannie Brice and I had been friends for many many years, and at her earthly passing, her fine son and daughter bid me speak—and I did, like so.

24. Eulogy for Fannie Brice. Temple Israel

MAY 31, 1951

I SPEAK FOR THE men and women in the theatrical business: the gang on 42nd Street and Broadway; for the crowds in front of Henrici's in the Loop in Chicago; for the bunch on the corners of Hollywood and Vine.

Ofttimes have I been chosen to speak so at the passing of a favorite son in the profession—and the toll of the last few years tugs cruelly at the strings of my heart. The poet Goethe once wrote a sonnet to which Tchaikowsky composed music—this is known to us as *None but the Lonely Heart*. But the meaning in its original tongue is more poignant which, translated from the German, means: "Only he who has known nostalgia knows my heartache." The older I get, the more I realize, as we all should, that all is vanity, all things go back from whence they came—and only words are left behind. I have stood and watched old friends, one by one, take their leave of this scene—and only words are left—words that become blurred as the tears fall on the charter of this, our generation. And now my hands fasten to my heart in lament for this all-too-soon exit from the scene of Fannie Brice. May the Lord please forgive me if this be blasphemy, but it seems all too soon.

And the speech from *As You Like It:* "All the world's a stage and all the men and women merely players" is not apt for this occasion. She was not permitted to run the gamut of life's fullest emotional parts—though she played the infant in the nurse's arms, and the school girl with shining morning face creeping like a snail unwillingly to school, and though she played the lover, sighing with the woeful ballad, and the Ziegfeld girl seeking the bubble reputation —she should have been kept longer on this stage to sit in the rocking chair with her grandchildren blissfully cooing on her lap . . . at least a little while longer. But the great Playwright of this ever-beginning, never-ending plot, the Master Director who so skillfully stages this tightly woven, disconnected spectacle of tragic nonsense, has planned it otherwise. And thus does her earthly career and her personal goodness live on only in fond memory. And it is not in the province of us transients to ask any questions, but only to believe that the play begins again and all the scenes are fully clarified—and that the curtain rises again.

Oft did I stand in the wings and hear her sing "Oh, my man I love him so, he'll never know . . ." And while this is a phrase in a hapless lover's melancholy roundelay, holy men of all races and creeds have often used this same phrase, and men of the cloth have put it in the mouth of God: " 'I love my man,' saith the Lord, 'he must know that I do.' " May this be consolation, though so tiny at the moment, to those who nestle close to Fannie, the fact that she does know now that Almighty God loves her. They must believe that—and we must believe that. If we do not, then we are only the dust that returneth. If we do believe, we, too, are God-like.

And so, Fannie, speaking for the men and women whose love was and is yours, I bid you *au revoir*—and I hope that your friends here in this holy house will share the thought that I shall try to keep in my mind when I take my leave of this pulpit. I shall not think, "Here lies Fannie Brice, stilled into silence from violent illness." I shall say over and over in my mind that "Fannie Brice, a fine American Jewess, a great artist and a devoted mother has gone up the road to her fathers"—and I shall say to my little girl-child, "Baby Snooks has gone to sleep."

I have spoken for the men and women in the theatrical business: the gang on 42nd Street and Broadway; for the crowds in front of Henrici's in the Loop in Chicago; for the bunch on the corner of Hollywood and Vine.

I shall now read the Twenty-Third Psalm written in the time of the shepherd King David.

Jeri, one of the sweetest memories of your early childhood I am sure, is going to be about your first playmate—a sweet little Negro child, Eunice.

You remember, she and her mother came to live at your house. Poor little thing, she had almost lost her right eye. The last time I saw her, however, she was quite grown, and while I don't remember asking about it, I think the sight of the eye had almost all come back. Isn't that wonderful?

Anyway, I remember us all listening to some records from Porgy and Bess: *"Summertime," "It Ain't Necessarily So," "Bess," "I Got Plenty of Nothin'," etc. And then I told you about the composer of those wonderful melodies, George Gershwin, and about the great love between him and his brother Ira, who wrote the poems to fit his melodies.*

It was not necessary, nor in key with the fun we were having, to tell you that Gershwin died in his late thirties—what a wonderful boy he was, and so chock full of talent—how after he composed "Rhapsody in Blue" he arose from the piano, walked to a canvas, and started to paint, for he was quite an artist as well.

On two occasions I spoke of him publicly. Once, at the Hollywood Bowl. Backed by the great symphony orchestra, great artists like Jolson, Fred Astaire, Lena Horne, Dinah Shore, and many others who sang his melodies up into the star-studded sky.

Then, some time later, I spoke at a memorial concert in Carnegie Hall in New York, to the accompaniment of Michel Piastro and his orchestra playing softly behind me. This is what I said:

25. George Gershwin Memorial
Speech. Carnegie Hall
1949

I HAVE COME HERE TO SPEAK about George Gershwin, and it is right that I speak because I was his friend. And in July, 1937, I spoke a eulogy in the great Hollywood Bowl in California under the heavens while the trees swayed to the memory of his music and the stars whispered his *Kaddish*. So be it.

The time: 1898. The place: New York City, America. More specifically, Grand Street on the lower east side. This was the birthplace of George Gershwin—and at the turn of the century he listened to the sounds outside his window, the voice of the boiling melting pot. The pounding of the El trains from the Bowery, the cries of the vendors on the sidewalks: "Pananas, Horanges, ets three for fiva cents." "*Noo veiber kaift-epis, bulbus, pomerancen.*" [Jargon: meaning—now, wives, buy something; potatoes, oranges, etc.] The voices of the Italian mothers from the tenements: "Hey, Tony, looka out you don't hurta youself."

The Irish cop walking his beat: "Get away from under that ice wagon or I'll take you to the stationhouse."

All this extra blueprint on the mind of little George, although he didn't quite know it at the time. A blueprint that later was to be transformed into some of the most creative music ever composed by an American. (*Rhapsody in Blue, Concerto in F, An American in Paris, Porgy and Bess*) —all monuments of American music. But for the moment let us stay in the sweet yesterday with the songs of Gershwin: those little offshoots of the early blueprint, the thirty-two-bar portrait of Gershwin's world.

George had a motto: "Music must reflect the spirit of the people and the times. My people are Americans . . . my time is today." In his early teens he was already following the courses he had charted for himself. He made one of his first public appearances before the Finley Club of the College of the City of New York at Christodora House on the east side, playing a song of his own. Ira Gershwin was a member of this club. And Ira always brought his kid brother. Later George became rehearsal pianist for the Victor Herbert-Jerome Kern show, *Miss 1917*. He went to work in Tin Pan Alley for Remick's. His tune "You, Just You-oo" was taken for a musical-comedy success of 1918, *Hitchy Koo*.

Nineteen-nineteen marked the turning point of his career. For one day, while riding on a Riverside Drive bus, a melody came to his mind, and a few days later, in collaboration with Irving Caesar, a song was born called "Swanee," a song sung with great success then by Al Jolson, and to this very day a song sung with great success by Al Jolson. The spirit of the nation has been captured by Gershwin in this song, and from then on he was on his way. He composed the music for musical plays like *The Midnight Whirl* and *A Dangerous Maid* and songs for *The Scandals of 1921*.

And in the midst of all this activity, he moved uptown and his reputation kept growing. Musicians of note called him not a song writer but "a new, promising, American composer."

In 1923 the French chanteuse, Eva Gauthier, sang his songs on the concert stage.

The year 1924 was a happy one. The Prince of Wales toured America. The spirit of romance, beauty, and beautiful girls was prevalent on Broadway. The roaring twenties roared forth its glamour with the Ziegfeld Follies, its Passing Shows, and the Scandals. Gershwin composed the music for many of the Scandals, and from these came the one-act play *135th Street* and the lovely melody "Somebody Loves Me." Then he wrote the score of *Lady Be Good*, which included the songs "Lady Be Good" and "Fascinating Rhythm." It is an oddity that the great torch song "The Man I Love" was also written for the play *Lady Be Good*, but it didn't seem to fit and was removed before the play opened on Broadway. Lady Louis Mountbatten, while visiting this country, heard it at a party and took it back to England with her and it scored a great success and is, to this day, sung and played everywhere, and is respected as the perfect model of the blues ballad.

The year 1924 removed from the scene the great Puccini of Italy and America's Victor Herbert, but American music continued to rise in stature, and people were beginning to sing and recite the songs of Rodgers and Hart, and the popular songs of the Gershwins became more profound with each composition. The melodies of George far removed from the bromidic tempo of Tin Pan Alley—and each of Ira's lyrics became more like a poem or a story. But at the end of that year George had an ambition realized as an American composer of great contributions when at Aeolian Hall, Paul Whiteman introduced "Rhapsody in Blue."

The sound of the city that George Gershwin first heard on Grand Street in New York and injected into his music was swelling into a roar that could be heard all over America: the roar of the twenties. Speed was the by-word. Sensationalism became a fetish, and fadism was rampant. In the midst of all this bustle Gershwin mirrored his times in melody. As musical comedies and motion pictures grew more emphatic, in their glorification of pleasure, Gershwin turned out one beautiful love song after another.

The roar went out of the twenties at the end of October in 1929. The bubble burst . . . millionaires became the middle class. The middle class became paupers. The ensuing panic sobered up an inebriated generation. The violent gyrations of the decade ground to a halt. But not George Gershwin. No, not George. He went right on composing music to fit the spirit of his people and his times. In his music the epoch found its reflection. One night in Boston he conducted the pre-Broadway tryout of *Strike Up the Band*. People left the theater humming one of its tunes, a tune of hope: "Soon."

Nineteen twenty-nine, with its overtones of frustration and unhappiness, got a shot in the arm from some of Gershwin's music. While Byrd was exploring the Antarctic and the major powers were signing the Kellogg-Briand Treaty, George was writing another Broadway hit called *Show Girl*. It featured the insinuating strains of "Liza."

By 1930 George Gershwin was making a fortune from his music. Whatever he touched pleased the many. The "Rhapsody," the Concerto, and "American in Paris" were played by all the symphony orchestras of the world. He had more than a score of hits on Broadway. Yet he remained essentially a cautious man, sure of himself, yes, but always trying to improve the quality of his art. From time to time he would devote himself to studying the various techniques of composition, but somehow he never could stay at it for long. He was constantly surrounded by the great and the near-great, giving as freely of his time to a schoolgirl asking for an interview as he would to a visiting ambassador. Still the melodies flowed from his pen. Nineteen-thirty was the year he wrote *Girl Crazy*, a score that bristled with striking rhythms: "Embraceable You," "I Got Rhythm," "Biding My Time," "But Not for Me."

Finally, in the winter of 1930, Hollywood offered George an immense sum to write the score for a picture starring Janet Gaynor and Charles Farrell called *Delicious*. It took only a few weeks for him to compose the tunes required. While in Hollywood George wrote his *Second Rhapsody*, but even more important than the *Second Rhapsody* was his collaboration that year with brother Ira, George Kaufman and Morris Ryskind on a new kind of musical comedy, a show that was the first to successfully introduce American satire into the field. It was called *Of Thee I Sing*. *Of Thee I Sing* was filled with the kind of humor and melody that America seemed psychologically ready for in 1932. Tunes like "Wintergreen for President" and "Who Cares?" filled the air from coast-to-coast, but the brightest, happiest moment from the score that put a political twist to moon and June, was "Love Is Sweeping the Country."

Things began to look up for the United States in 1933. Franklin D. Roosevelt began his first term in office. This began an era of more tolerant principles and new ideas. Everyone was talking about "Technocracy" and the Century of Progress Exposition in Chicago. Folks were reading *Anthony Adverse* and *Life Begins at Forty* and jamming movie theaters to see Walt Disney's *Three Little Pigs*. While Jerome Kern was being acclaimed for *Music in the Air* and

Roberta, George was composing still another show: *Let 'em Eat Cake.* Though the show is almost forgotten, everyone remembers the languid hit from the score, "Mine."

By now George had come a long way from the lower east side. He was considered by many as the most important American composer of the century, as well as a top writer of the popular hits that mirrored his people and the times. He composed for the movies, the theater, and the concert hall. He played the piano wherever he went and took up conducting. He started work in 1933 on *Porgy and Bess;* 1934 was spent touring the country conducting concerts of popular music. Nineteen thirty-five saw the première of *Porgy and Bess,* the most important contribution by an American composer in our time. By now he was an international figure. In 1936 he returned to Hollywood where he scored the Fred Astaire picture *Shall We Dance* with its lovely melody, "They Can't Take That Away from Me."

During the cool of a summer evening in 1937, while feverishly working on the music for the *Goldwyn Follies,* Gershwin collapsed suddenly and mysteriously. It was diagnosed as a slight nervous breakdown. He recovered partly and went back to his work. But not for long. And at ten thirty-five on the morning of July 11, at the peak of his career, in the bloom of his manhood, with his melodies on the lips and in the throats and in the hearts of the nation, the Power that is not to be challenged in this life saw fit to take him away from us and, as it was since their childhood days, brother Ira was at his side. So be it. *Baruch Dion Emeth.* Blessed is the Righteous Judge.

To speak of George Gershwin, past or future, is to speak of the past and future of a singing brook. He was—he is— he will be. His heart ceased to beat on July 11, 1937; the fingers that caressed the white and the dark keys are stilled.

But the music goes on. And so it has become a great warm, living memory—a memory of a son of man who has fulfilled a great destiny in a great manner, in a great country that gave him and gives all men equal opportunity.

Long live Gershwin.

Long live America.

Jerilynn, your name is rather an unusual one. I never heard it before. Your mother suggested it for you.

All reports before you entered the world were to the effect that you were to be a boy, and therefore your mother and I agreed to name you after James J. Walker, one of my closest and dearest friends, and your godfather. You were to be James J. Jessel. But nature rewrote you, so we came upon Jerilynn by combining James with the name of a close friend of your mother's called Lynn.

Your godfather was one of the greatest personalities this country has ever known. Though one or more books have been written about him, they never even scratched the surface, and instead of word-picturing him as a man who might have reached the greatest heights as public servant, humanitarian, with a most prolific mind in the study of law and public speaking, as well as benefactor toward mankind, he was written about as a happy-go-lucky good-time Charlie who, as mayor of New York City, allowed his friends and politicians to play havoc with City Hall.

He started falling from grace politically when the dollar fell and the crashes came and conditions brought about investigations of all kinds. And during the Seabury investigation in New York, he was forced into resignation by the smallest of things, but that nevertheless could be called "malfaisance in office."

It is still believed by some that he took a great deal of money from the coffers of the city of New York, whereas, in reality, he was a poor man almost immediately after he left office. There are few of us who know just how badly in need of money Jimmy was: Charlie Silver, Ed Mulrooney, Dr. Newman, and myself, one or two more. He died poor in worldly goods, but rich in everything else.

One night, after a tour of speech-making together, we made a pact, he and I. If and when one or the other would pass away, he would speak for me and I for him. During his last illness, however, he was taken back into the heart of the church, and was buried from the great St. Patrick's Cathedral in New York with the highest Mass, at which no layman could take part. I held services for him in California, via radio transcription, and these are the words I used—and the only reason I don't have the words of the other speakers is because they don't have them on paper as I do.

26. Radio Tribute to James J. Walker

Jessel: (Comes in on organ music: "Give My Regards to Broadway.") Among the friends of James J. Walker, who left this scene but a few days ago and all too soon, there were those whom he would have wanted to be at the side of his casket before it left St. Patrick's Cathedral in New York. I wanted so much to be there but was prevented because of time, distance, and the elements. It is fitting that I speak over the radio of him, for I had the privilege of being closer to Jim than any of my contemporaries or anyone in my business—the amusement business. One morning after Jim and I had spoken from the pulpit in Temple Emmanuel at the passing of a fellow New Yorker, Joseph Le Blang, we made a rather curious pact, grave yet gay, never dreaming that it would come into effect so soon. I was to speak at his bier, or he at mine. Although I could not carry out my part, the highest Mass was read for Jim, which is much more consoling than anything that could come from the mouths of a legion of minstrels. I therefore take this opportunity to speak an extra word or two. I shall then introduce a fellow New Yorker. Shakespeare, in his tragedy *Julius Caesar*, contrasts the virtues of Cassius, the lean one, and Anthony, the stout. Of Cassius he says: "He is learned, he is observing, he reads the hearts and minds of men." Of Anthony: "He is gay, he is heroic, he loves plays and music, and he sleeps well." All these are requisites of a citizen of the world. Such was Jimmy Walker. Or, if you will bear with me, may I say— such *is* Jimmy Walker, for I like to believe and I want to believe what a little old lady in New England has said—a simple old lady if you will —a sainted old lady, if you please—that there is no such thing as death, what seems so is transition. Jim Walker's voice of good will can never be hushed, for it is the heartbeat of the city of New York. Though he leaves no son, seven million people and their sons will remember him and forever sing his praises and chant his *Kaddish.* A stone's throw away from where Jimmy was born did there come into the light of the world a boy who as each year goes by, finds himself reflecting more credit upon himself and to America. He is known and beloved by everyone. We call each other brother. I am privileged now to bring to the microphone—Eddie Cantor.

Cantor: (Speaks one minute and sings a chorus of "East Side, West Side"—organ accompaniment.)

Jessel: This is Georgie Jessel again to let those who are younger and therefore not cognizant or aware of Jimmy's true greatness—to let them know of his tolerance toward all people and all religions. He once said in a speech that believing in God was like going to

Buffalo. There are many railroads for those who really want to go to Buffalo. There are many ways of believing in God. With that thought in mind I am privileged to bring to the microphone three distinguished clergymen . . .

Methodist Minister: (two minutes)

Rabbi: (two minutes)

Priest: (two minutes)

Jessel: It is fitting indeed that one of America's greatest singers of popular songs should now render for you one written by one of America's most colorful men. Dick Haymes now sings Jimmy Walker's "Will You Love Me in December as You Do in May?"

Haymes: (Sings verse and chorus.)

Jessel: This is Georgie Jessel again, speaking to you from Hollywood on a night in November and "The moon for sorrow will not show its rays." And early November finds New York with falling leaves on Central Park and falling tears on Broadway. William Morris—George M. Cohan—Jimmy Walker. All have gone from the Roaring Forties. During this melancholy November all have gone from the Big Street, leaving it as sad as they so often made it happy—thus does our moment of tribute end, but only for the moment. *Au revoir,* Jimmy. Rest ye fair, sweet Jimmy, with the blessings of millions and of these few gathered here—three of God's ministers and three old friends. Good-by for the time being— Good-by, kid, Father Knickerbocker's arms are empty, for you were his truly begotten son.

Honey, I've written you all about the time I joined the Gus Edwards Vaudeville Acts, and his Music Publishing Company—but I never told you much about him.

He was a genius, if there ever was one. He composed such beautiful melodies, and yet he could not read a note of music, nor could he play the piano very well. He would hit a few chords and let his left hand slide down to a base note, and it sometimes would land in an ashtray. But just think, honey, how his songs are remembered! Even you and all your school chums sing "School Days," and his melodies are used several times daily on radio-TV as theme songs for programs such as "My Merry Oldsmobile"—and "Tammany" the Barbasol tune, and Lord knows how many other songs most of which he composed in collaboration with the poet, Will D. Cobb.

He was a very poor businessman. Heaven knows what would have happened to him and his house had it not been for Mrs. Gus Edwards—Lillian—a remarkable woman blessed with the virtue of seeing and hearing no evil and further blessed by reaching her late seventies with all the faculties of a much younger woman.

From his company, in my time, there were quite an alumni: the Marx Brothers, Eddie Cantor, Walter Winchell, Mervyn Le Roy, Georgie Price, Lila Lee, the Duncan Sisters, and much later on, Hildegarde, Ray Bolger, and others.

Most all of them came to say good-by to him in the little chapel on Santa Monica Boulevard, and I spoke for them as follows:

27. Eulogy for Gus Edwards

Since the Author has seen fit to write this sad scene, my part is well cast. I sat on Gus Edward's knee while he played the piano and taught me to sing in 1909. But I speak not only for myself but for the entire Gus Edwards' alumni when I say that everything gentle about us was taught to us by Gus, for he was all that was gentle. And while there is no son left behind to chant his *Kaddish*, his memory will not die as long as we, his pupils, have voices and the power to speak. Although not given the supposedly allotted threescore and ten, the sadness of his seeming passing from the scene is lighter because of the joy that surrounded him in all the years up to his last illness. The joy of hearing the nation sing his songs, the joy of singing them himself to the plaudits of millions. But greatest of all, the God-given joy of having the most devoted life partner that any man has ever known. It is of she that tarries behind that I must speak, for it is she that has to be reconciled. For it is only the lonely years that are long. Only the lonely years. Oh, if ever there were tenderness and understanding between two people, such there was between Gus and his Lily. No virtue too small to compliment; no fault too great that was not forgiven. Once, while standing at the tomb of Abelard and Eloise in Père Lachaise, I was told the legend—that these two young lovers, taken away in their youth, were destined never to part. Such shall be the case of Mr. and Mrs. Gus Edwards, for I believe as a simple old lady in New England has said—simple old lady, if you wish; sainted old lady, if you will—there is no such thing as death. What seems so is transition, and I would sing for sweet Lillian the lyric of Machushla. "Death is a dream and love lives for aye." And so I beg of you, sweet devoted wife, hold fast to the thought that you have not tasted the last kiss of your beloved.

It is said that the soul of a man goes to the heaven that he'd dreamed about. His particular heaven. If so, I can see in the offing the heaven that Gus must have often dreamed of. Thousands upon thousands of happy kids listening to him singing the verse of a song and joining in the chorus with him. For neither time nor age has diminished the sweetness of the melody nor the sentiment of the lyric.

> School days, school days,
> Dear old Golden Rule days;
> Readin', an' writin', an' 'rithmetic,
> Taught to the tune of a hick'ry stick;
> You were my queen in calico;
> I was your bashful barefoot beau;
>   You wrote on my slate
>   "I love you, Joe,"
> When we were a couple of kids.

The early Hebrew fathers handed down to us this law: that at all times sing the praises of the Lord. At all times sanctify His goodness. Praise the Lord in times of great sadness and alike in moments of joy. At the birth of a newborn; at the passing of a man. Thus do we salute tradition. Hear O Israel the Lord our God, the Lord is one. Blessed is the righteous Judge. Thus do we salute Gus Edwards— all that was gentle. Amen.

*Jeri, I know how much you admire Clark Gable,
and how handsome you think he is—and you're right.*

*But the best-looking man, in my opinion, whom I
ever saw on stage or screen, was John Barrymore. He
was the most illustrious son of this Royal Family of
actors and actresses. He had a million friends and
maybe two enemies: sometimes himself and sometimes the dreaded disease of insecurity.*

*I was not able to be with him at the end. But a short
time later the New York newspaper, PM, asked me to
write a piece about him. Here it is:*

28. Eulogy for John Barrymore

WHAT PRICE GIRDLE?

WHEN THE LATE, great John Barrymore passed
away, like nearly everyone who loves the theater, I was
deeply affected. And when one night there was an auction in
Hollywood where his personal effects were sold, I wrote to a
group of people in New York and sent them the following:

I know you'll hate me for this, but the weather out here
is divine, the temperature is always around eighty, and
just cool enough at night to have the blanket nearby, if not
in actual use. The quiet in Beverly Hills is almost majestic,
and there are more stars in the skies than there are at Metro
or Twentieth Century-Fox, regardless of what they say in
their ads. My day has been most pleasant. I stayed home

and sat in the garden, saluting the works of nature and the wonders of the Racing Form.

This is the first day in the fortnight I've spent out here in Double-Feature-by-the-Sea when I didn't go out, thereby ducking the daily hisses I usually get from some of the folks out here who refuse to believe that actors should speak their mind or venture public opinion. All this was forgotten, in this lovely day of sweet summer, until my eyes found themselves on the evening newspaper of a few days' vintage. Then, just as a tiny dark cloud sets itself before the sun, so did a tiny ad in the Hollywood and Los Angeles papers darken the day for me and for those others who allow themselves to be sensitive out here in the land of sky-blue salaries. For this advertisement read:

> The personal belongings of the bankrupt estate of John Barrymore will be sold at auction; items included are: hats, ties, shoes, pajamas, suits, and his girdle.

I pictured it like so . . . over the "going . . . going . . . gone" of the auctioneer, it seemed to me there was a sinister voice whispering, "That's it; clown it up, clown it up; don't even let him rest in dignity."

The only saving grace of this motley, maudlin scene was that, somewhere in the wings, I know Barrymore laughed like hell. This writer is one, of but a few, whose picture of John Barrymore is a montage of the finest things in the American theater: in *Hamlet*, in *Justice*, in *The Jest*, in *Resurrection*—not as a comic foil to sell ice cream over the radio.

When, in fancy, I hear him speak, Shakespeare is in the prompter's box, not Joe Miller. And yet, the pity of it, Iago, the pity of it, that the secondhand ties, the old rakish hats, the worn pajama coats, and the girdle, yet, of this great prince of the theater (mad, if you will; genius, if you please) should be placed under the auction hammer, so that a hundred cheap gags could be told between bids.

Surely there is someone, close enough to him to love him, who could have and should have quietly purchased the rags, lock, stock, and barrel, and given them to the Actor's Fund, or any theatrical guild, so that actors who have long since tasted defeat might sip again a tiny bit of triumph by proudly saying, "See this hat, see this jacket I'm wearing? I got it from John Barrymore." The whole package probably sold for less than a thousand dollars—a mere *tsimis* here in close-up town. Even not-too-rich me, had I known, would have given the wherewithal to bind the bargain.

Last night was the end of the auction; there was very little left to sell: a few bow ties, a few bottoms of pajamas, maybe a pipe. Then, thank the gods, the ad reading, "The personal belongings of the bankrupt estate of John Barrymore will be sold at auction," will rest in the dark files of the newspapers. Maybe some night the letters which formed the ad will be ashamed and jump from the page screaming, "We should never, never have got together in the first place." And, perhaps some kind printer's devil will bring them together so that they will read: "We are sorry for what we said; we are only words, but we loved John Barrymore—for we were always so sweet when we came from his mouth."

We know that when, near the last, he played the clown, he needed the money badly. He was ill, and, to live or not to live, that was the question. Wherever he is, may he stand to his full height, even though *sans* ties, *sans* pajamas, *sans* pipe, *sans* hat, *sans* girdle, *sans* everything.

Dearest daughter:

This chapter is about words and thoughts, and though I had hardly any schooling, I began reading at nine. First, the five-cent novels of the heroic Liberty Boys of '76, then some actual history of our country, and then, boom, before you know it, I was reading a magazine called Pearson's, edited by Frank Harris.

In this magazine Mr. Harris himself wrote word portraits of famous people. Twenty-five years later we were to become close friends. He even came on as an extra in a motion picture I made, called Lucky Boy, in which I sang the song "My Mother's Eyes," which is still selling copies, and from which I am buying you a birthday present.

After reading Pearson's magazine, I read some of the romantic novels, and when I was around fifteen, I started reading poetry: Laurence Hope, Emily Dickinson, Edna Millay, and finally got to A. E. Housman— and I keep reading him again and again, one poem particularly that ends like so:

> But men at whiles are sober
> And they think by fits and starts
> And if they think they fasten
> Their hands upon their hearts . . .

You know something? I hope someday you will take to writing poetry. I remember once, when you were seven, you handed me the title that you were going to write a poem about. It was "The noise, the song, and the dream." That's about as far as you got. Well, I too have started a lot of poems that never got much further. So keep thinking that thoughts are things, and here are some of mine.

29. Cabbages and Catechism

W HEN I WAS YOUR AGE, JERILYNN, I got a daily
thrill walking down Broadway, often with a tin make-up box
under my arm, so that everyone would know that I was an
actor going to work. And to make sure there would be no
mistake, there was always a little pink grease paint around
the edge of my high, stiff collar, so that my brother players
would know I couldn't have been laying off very long. I
remember so well standing around Times Square, trying to
get into conversation with older actors, and I can remember
two big signs, one on a building and one a theater: "O'Connor & Goldberg, for the best shoes" and "Cohan and Harris,
Presenting the Best Plays."

And I can remember a dark-skinned shoe-black who used
to sing, "Just because my hair is curly, that's why they call
me Shine . . ."

More than forty years have gone by since then, and it is
all so different. O'Connor & Goldberg—Cohan and Harris
—like the signs on the building and on the theater—have
gone, and that happy partnership of the Irish-American
and the Jewish-American is no longer Broadway talk . . .
although I am sure that if you sauntered down Broadway
now, Jerilynn, you'd hear lots about McCarthy and Cohn,
and as an added starter, Schine.

I know Senator Joe, Roy, and David all fairly well, and

firstly, I in no way concur that the senator from Wisconsin is a villain, that he is dreaming of a dictatorship, or that he is anti-Semitic. Politically, during the last presidential campaign (Eisenhower-Stevenson), I was the first one in my business who had the courage to attack his methods as far as the campaign was concerned. At Madison Square Garden, before presenting Governor Stevenson, Senator Lehman, and others, I said, "I know that most of you are tired of hearing political speeches. I heard one last night that was a cuckoo. It was made by the senator from Wisconsin, Joseph Goebbels—oh, oh, excuse me—I meant McCarthy."

The garden-filled Democrats screamed in applause. A short time after that I met the senator. We kidded about it, and I found him to be a man with a most ingratiating personality . . . at least that is how he hit me. I believe him to be completely sincere in fighting communism everywhere, whether it looms up large or whether there is the tiniest hint. While I certainly don't approve of his methods, I think that many of us in condemning often, the vicious attitude of a mean cop, we are inclined to forget the culprit and the crime, for surely if there had been no suspicion regarding the army dentist, there would have been no insults to General Zwicker . . .

Of course, we must remember that were there no such thing as communism, there would be no such thing as some people call McCarthyism. There are some who have met the senator through TV newsreels and such who don't like his personality, and no doubt he does rub some folks the wrong way, no matter what he does. I remember once I was in a show with a very temperamental performer, who is well known for not being able to get along with anyone. And one day a fellow said to me, "Have you had any fights with Jimsy?" I said, "Oh no. He's all right—unless you go out of your way to upset him like saying 'Good morning,' or 'Isn't it a nice day?' "

McCarthy's bitterness in the campaign attacks, if they are not to be completely forgiven, must be tolerated. Unfortunately some members of both parties still seem convinced that "all is fair, etc. . . ." And if we don't forgive Republican McCarthy for attacking Senator Tydings undeservedly, we certainly should not forgive Democrat Mitchell for attacking the personal integrity of President Eisenhower.

As to that big show, the Army *vs.* McCarthy shindig, it seems to me the Army had a good case against him because the good work of the senator in trying to turn out those who are lacking in Americanism was completely undone by his public condemnation of the heads of the Army, which violently hurt our prestige in Europe, the man on the street in France and Italy and other countries embellishing the newspaper headlines even further, and actually believing that our armed forces were full of Communists, which everyone knows is not the case. The Army's case should have been that McCarthy was hurting the morale of our people in America and abroad, and that his methods must be changed and his type of investigation stopped. But they never came into court with that case. The whole thing seemed to be about what Private Schine was doing in between eating big steaks over the week end, while he was so sorely missed at Camp Dix where he would have been watching a movie on Sunday night. It reminded me of a man I knew who found his wife in *flagrante delicto* on several occasions. He found her in the arms of the chauffeur, the chauffeur's father, and a lodge member of his father's who had stopped by to pick up an umbrella. And so, with this direct evidence he made up his mind to divorce her, but came into court saying he wished to divorce his wife on the grounds that she always

sang "Wait Till the Sun Shines, Nellie" at breakfast and that
he preferred a newer song.

As for Roy Cohn, I met him through interesting circumstances. I received a phone call from the international columnist Leonard Lyons late one night. He said, "Come over
to the Stork Club and meet Roy Cohn. He is going to make
a speech tomorrow and attack Senator Herbert Lehman.
From what I know about it, Cohn's speech should be tem-
pered, and I think you could help." I met Roy, and we had
quite a talk, in which, of course, I defended the record and
personal integrity of the New York senator and told Roy he
would get nowhere in attacking the senator in that manner.
Roy Cohn is a smart young man. He listened to Lyons and
myself, followed our suggestion, and took much that was
venom and in error from his speech. I understand that at
the age of thirteen he was mentally equipped to pass the bar
examination and enter all courts of law. How you get that
brilliant so early is a hard thing to figure out, any more than
you can have the answer to a kid of seven being a chess
player or a violin virtuoso—but we know there are such
things. I don't believe that Cohn is through. On the contrary, I believe he will make his presence felt through the
years in the courts of law.

Why and what David Schine was doing in all this, I'll
never know. And why the administration allowed thousands
of dollars to be spent and so much valuable time lost in trying to find out day after day where he bought his shoes, what
the color was of the hair of the girl he danced with, is something that should be talked about in the coming election
campaign.

Schine is a very attractive young man, with a good mind,
and I cannot understand why he ever made that silly trip to
Europe where the best he could get was the worst of it, as

the events which followed have proved. I wish his smart dad and his beautiful mother had more influence over him.

Sometimes I wish you, my child, could walk down the happy Broadway that I did, and see the big signs of O'Connor & Goldberg and Cohan and Harris, and listen to the little boy sing, "That's why they call me Shine," instead of seeing it the way it is now, with people glaring at each other as they talk about McCarthy-Cohn-Schine. But it is not their fault. If there were no Commies, Joe McCarthy could still be a handsome Captain of the Marines, Cohn might be the attorney of the Schine Hotels, and David would still be doing what he was doing over the week end he was on leave from camp.

> *I Believe* "Not till the fire is dying in the grate
>   look we for any kinship with the stars."
>
> *George Meredith*

I have one of the largest collections of *materia religiosa.* As to Judaism and Christianity, I have studied ever so much of the letter even though I often fail to feel the spirit, and I am conversant with nearly all that has been written which is saluted as fact. That which fancy has fashioned is up to whoever would believe, for whatever you think is good is sufficient, and only that which transpires in your mind is reality; all that is probability to you may be real to other minds.

Of the religion of the Hebrews and Christianity which followed some three thousand years later, I dare not delve into too deeply in a book such as this, which is light reading matter. We know from what has been writ on stone or on parchment that the word "Hebrew" is a derivation of the word *hivaru* from an ancient Semitic language, and meant "those from the other side; those from over the river." And we know that a group of shepherd people and their kin suddenly emerged near what is now called Israel some six thousand years ago. Despite the fact that these Hebraic tribes were dispersed, their code of ethics handed down by Moses made them one in believing in an Invisible God who created mankind and promised salvation on earth if the laws, or the Torah, were adhered to. Because of circumstances which prevailed in these early days, many things were added: rituals, sacrifice, strange laws that today seem nothing more than superstitious and fanatic. Through the years there has been a happy compromise. Today there exists a code of religious belief that is more dignified, intelligent, and soul-inspiring for those of the Jewish people whose desire it is to honestly believe. And in order to do this, it is not particularly necessary to salute any of the older customs unless you wish to do it out of memory of Grandpa, and because you will never forget that look in his eyes as he came home and carefully folded his praying shawl. But a student can very early learn that most of the Mosaic laws having to do with food and the body were laid down only because of sanitary conditions.

As to Christianity, if men would but follow its tenets, the world would forever be at peace and in harmony. Whether or not Hillel said the things accredited to the Galilean Jeshua (named Jesus by the Greeks some one hundred years after his passing) this is of no importance. And the fact that there is actually no written word left for us, and that most of the Apostles have written only from hearsay, and that Saulus (Paul) came forty years later and preached what he saw in a dream, cannot take away from the truth that Christianity is good. And we must further salute the fact that all civilization, scientifically and artistically, has been furthered by those of the Christian faith, even though outnumbered many times by Moslems and the godless who attempt to control the destinies of mankind, today. Perhaps this is because the Moslem goes high to his minaret and looks toward Mecca for the answer to everything. The average Christian or Jew, if and when he says his prayers, quickly goes about living a creative life and believes that God helps those who help themselves; and that he who is diligent in business shall stand before kings.

To those of the Jewish faith who are interested in the study of their own religion, or to those who find themselves lacking in knowledge of it, I would advise to read the Sermons and Articles of Rabbis Magnin and Nussbaum, of the Los Angeles, California, Temples, Emmanuel and Israel.

A New Art—And How to Perfect It

Among the things that actors, actresses, and entertainers have to learn daily in addition to each new technical gimmick that comes up, is how to answer a heckler; someone who is either stewed or disorderly in a public place where the artist is endeavoring to entertain.

This has become a most important talent to acquire in the last few years. For, because of the free entertainment on radio and TV, where the artist cannot answer back, there has developed an irreverence which nearly always arises about something that the public gets for nothing. So that the children who answer back the TV, and often rub popcorn on the actors' faces, grow up to be just as fresh toward live performers later on in life. And when they interrupt the artist, the artist must be ready to say something like Joe E. Lewis does: "You can go home now, your cage has been cleaned." Or: "I saw you before, I am sure—under a microscope." Or: "Bless your alcoholic little heart."

Nearly all of today's comics who play the night clubs, benefits, etc., have to have such a routine. In the few times

I tried my hand at night-club entertaining (and not too successfully), I was bothered once by a fellow who had been drinking too much, and it sort of stunned me. I said to him, "I know that there are a lot of things to say to you that the other comics have right at the tip of their tongue, but unfortunately I don't know any of these answers to people like yourself, because, you see, this is the first time I've been heckled by anybody." But once I did have the right answer. This was at a dinner given in Dallas, Texas, at which I had to introduce the great American Wendell Willkie. This was after he had been defeated for the presidency, and while I was warmly introducing Mr. Willkie, some fellow got up and yelled, "He couldn't make it before, and he won't make it now." And then I suddenly remembered the line from a poem by the late Arthur Caesar, and I said, "My friend, don't be so sure of that. Remember what the Scriptures tell us: God's delay doesn't mean God's denial."

For Those Who've Had to Take It

There are many men who, because they continue to be in love, or because of something or other, take a terrible beating throughout the years from a wife or a sweetheart, and nearly always cause their friends and close kin to exclaim, "How can he stand it? Why does he do it? He should have given her up long ago, etc." Maybe it is not love, maybe it is not pity, maybe the answer might be in this: Sometimes imperfection is captivating or sometimes it is the joy of self-sacrifice. By everybody else's standard, this is stupid and means nothing, but by your standard it does. It is stupid to the rest of the world, but satisfying to you . . .

Doodling with Words:

A portrait of the word "horror": You are motoring through Germany. You go through wonderful little villages, clean, white, and prosperous—and suddenly, you come upon Buchenwald or Dachau . . .

Kindliness: If your girl has but one eye, look at her profile.

Advice to screen writers: Biographies should not be done on the screen until the subject matter has left this life long enough to be lied about. The scenario writer dare not be contemporary with the undertaker.

Note on "What to Say" after a speaker who has been rather corny: "You can tell a woman is growing old by the lines on her neck; you can tell a man is growing old by the lines that come from his lips."

About a certain motion picture producer: He minds his own business at the top of his voice.

About a certain TV star: He has the ego of a rooster who actually believes that it is his crowing which brings on the dawn . . .

At the finish of a breakfast TV show, with an all-women audience:
Have the organ play "I Love You Truly" and say: "Whatever becomes of the little pictures that old folks leave behind—pictures of their mothers, their dads, brothers, sisters, relations, and friends—and all of them gone from the scene, faces that don't belong to the living, for no one is left to

whom they mean anything. Poor little faded pictures—memories looking for a heart to rest upon."

Optimism

The gag-man Barney Dean, dying at the age of fifty, whispering to Bob Hope, "Have you got any message you want me to give to Jolson?"

Pessimism

Julius Tannen, seventy-six years of age, hale, hearty, mind brilliantly alert: "There's very little that we can get out of life. If a child dies, it is buried under three feet of ground. If he lives to be old, he is buried under six feet of ground. So, the most you can get out of life is three feet . . ."

That Old Gang of Mine

Groucho, Danny Thomas, Holtz, Harpo, Holzman, and other comics whose elbows rest on the round table at Hillcrest, were listening to George Burns do a complete routine about supposed escapades of mine. He can make up more lies and make them more amusing than a hundred Barons Münchhausen—but this day, upon being asked why he showed up late for golf, he said he had been with me as I made a recording of my own eulogy, to be played at my passing.

I was kidded and ribbed about this for some time, for some people believed it not as another one of Burns' comic inventions but as a real fact.

However, I have written my epitaph, and as I shall close my life with it, thus do I close this printed page:

I TELL YOU HERE FROM THE SHADES
IT IS ALL WORTH WHILE.

October 22, 1954

CONFESSIONAL

Well, Miss thirteen-year-old-today, here's a book for you. It comes with your other birthday presents. The raincoat won't be around long—you'll probably grow out of it by next year; the little ring will have to be enlarged; and the radio which you can carry over your shoulder I'm sure you'll lose someplace; or perhaps even before its tubes are burned out, there'll be a new one invented which you can carry in your mouth or wear on your finger.

But I don't think you'll lose this book—at least I hope not. Although I don't think it'll adorn the shelves of the fastidious, in close proximity to Carlyle, Hardy, and Victor Hugo, it might find itself a permanent home with the folks who like to talk about how well they know show people. And of course I am sure it will be kept by most of the people who are mentioned in it. Everybody keeps books they're mentioned in, no matter what the contents.

But it's important to me, because there's been love for you in my mind and heart in preparing it. You're my only kin, you're the only thing that's happened in my life that seems to have an untainted beauty about it . . . with the exception of words that I've read. Every place else that I've searched for beauty, I found it not, for I know now that I've looked in the wrong places. For often there's been a cheapness in my thinking which has stunted me in everything I've attempted—except in the budgeting of words. As to the rest, I'm not too proud of myself. I have made so many mistakes and lost much character looking for luxury, just to save face and hide the insecurity that lurked behind my eyes . . .

Here's your book—here's my hand. Go forward and I'll go a little of the way with you. You're young and strong, and the tree of life beckons you to climb its branches. Reach high, high, higher . . . higher.

SO BE IT.